The Three Faces of Nellie

The Real Story Behind
Laura Ingalls Wilder's "Nellie Oleson"

Robynne Elizabeth Miller

DEDICATION

This one has got to be utterly, completely, and wholeheartedly dedicated to my beloved husband. Three books in to this crazy writing journey, and not only has he refrained from kicking me to the curb, but he's actually joined me in my obsessiveness. His love, patience, and support would have been enough to grant him super-hero status, but he's gone beyond: researching, editing, brain-storming, and much, much more.

So, this one's for you, SLE. Well, for both of us.

Thank you for the encouragement and the help.
Could not have done it without you.

I love you immeasurably.

CONTENTS

ACKNOWLEDGMENTS

I've said it before: Nothing worthwhile is ever accomplished without a community of support. And this project is certainly no exception.

I'm incredibly lucky to have such a community of family and friends. Your encouragement, tolerance, and flexibility has allowed me the time and bandwidth to complete this weighty project. Thank you all for your love and patience. It's meant the world to me.

And to both my writing tribe and the informal fraternity of historical researchers, well, you have been instrumental in the quality, depth, and value of this book. Without your tireless efforts to help discover and substantiate facts, and make sure that information was presented in a sentient manner, this resource would not be what it is. Thank you all!

I would particularly like to thank the staff of the Multnomah County Central Library in Portland, OR; Ruby Fry-Matson, of the Tillamook County Pioneer Museum; Frank McLean, of the Yakima Valley Genealogical Society; and Skip Buhler, of the Friends of Historic Forest Grove. Your assistance and research efforts provided some invaluable information, for which I am extremely grateful.

Finally, my biggest, best, and most hearty "thanks" go to Ian, who led the research behind this project. Ian has poured countless hours into "The Three Faces of Nellie," WAY beyond his job description, and mostly just because he wanted to do Nellie justice. Once brought on to the project, Ian quickly caught the "Nellie" vision and turned out some of the finest research we have on these women to date. Not only that, he's one of the kindest, most honorable, and, without a doubt, funniest men I've ever met. It has been an absolute pleasure to work with you, Ian. And if anyone has need of a top-notch historical researcher/genealogist, Ian has my highest recommendation. Part genealogist, part detective, part historian, and part bloodhound, he's just the best. (and I'm serious . . . if you're in need of his copious skills, contact me at robynne@robynnemiller.com.)

Thank you, Ian . . . job well done.

A Note to Readers

The *Three Faces of Nellie* was a labor of love. For Laura's writing. For the brave pioneers who settled the United States. And even for Nellie, herself. We tried in this biography to faithfully honor the legacy of each.

It's important to note that historical research is an ever-evolving discipline. With new technology, we have unprecedented access to historical documents of all kinds. We can, for the first time, sit in our living rooms and peruse an actual copy of a census taken a hundred and fifty years ago. We can see the beautiful handwriting. We can sense the history.

But mistakes were made: Last names were misspelled, nicknames were used, numbers were transposed, and some information was even intentionally incorrect. These were documents recorded by humans, and there were human errors made. A lot of them.

So, in *The Three Faces of Nellie*, we have done our best to check, re-check, and cross-check our information. Where we remained uncertain, we've noted it, and where there were discrepancies between accepted material and newly discovered data, we've tried to outline how they connect with, or contradict, each other.

We hope this has resulted in the most comprehensive overview of Nellie Owens, Genevieve Masters, and Estella Gilbert to date. But we know that even more information can still come to light. And we hope it does! If anyone has the personal diary of these three ladies, we'd LOVE to take a peek!

THE MAKING OF THE NELLIES

Never in the history of literature has there ever been a character so hated and yet so mesmerizing as Nellie Oleson! Of course, there's Peter Pan's Captain Hook, the White Witch in Narnia, and Captain Ahab's Moby Dick, just to name a few. . .but how many of them have a line of memorabilia that stretches from lunch boxes to t-shirts, coffee mugs to shot glasses? Not many, that's for sure. But Nellie does. Oh, yes, Nellie does!

Laura Ingalls Wilder's *Little House on the Prairie* series is, undisputedly, a literary phenomenon. With more than sixty million (MILLION!) copies sold in more than one hundred countries over the past eighty-plus years, these classics surpassed everyone's initial expectations, and continue to delight endless new generations of readers. In the beautifully written pages of Laura's semi-autobiographical stories, we got to make delicious yellow butter with Ma, help Pa with his leather door-hinges, and pick unusually aromatic prairie vi'lets with the girls.

And, secretly, we got to hate snooty Nellie Oleson, too.

We've all had some kind of "Nellie" in our lives. Someone who made us feel ugly, or poor, or stupid, or, well, *less-than* in some way. Laura's "Nellie" did all that and more. Unlike most of us, however, fictional Laura had the chance to get even with her "Nellie." We may never have had the opportunity to do so with ours (and probably shouldn't have, anyway), but in the *Little House* books, we got to giggle at stuck-on leeches, grab bags of candy out of her hands and deposit them in their rightful owner's, and watch a dashing buggy come around the corner, ready for a Nellie-less Sunday drive. These scenes were enormously satisfying to anyone who ever felt marginalized in any way.

While the *Little House* series was based on Laura's own life, true fans know that Laura used a lot of fictional techniques, and made a lot of bold narrative choices, that fuzzed the edges of strict biography. Not that we mind, of course. The characters she created and the stories she told captured the spirit of the pioneer experience, as well as our hearts. But the fact remains: Laura employed several descriptive techniques to tighten, drive, and enhance her prairie stories, and the creation of a composite Nellie Oleson was one of her most masterful.

It's no secret that Laura combined real-life people to craft the character of Nellie. Three, in fact. From this composite, an almost perfect, stereotypical arch-nemesis was born: pretty, willowy, snooty, and ever-so-fun to foil. But as wonderful as it was to hate Nellie, no person is ever all good or all bad, are they? Yet we didn't really get to see any redeeming side to that golden-haired, beautifully dressed rival of Laura in the books.

So, what's the real story?

It's as interesting and complicated as real life can be. And it's obvious that when you get to know the real "Nellies," you'll discover that some historical truths were slightly exaggerated for dramatic effect. You'll also notice that there were some awfully good reasons for Laura to dislike the real "Nellies" in her life, too. But here's something intriguing. . .in discovering the three real women behind the one fictional character, you'll find out that Laura, herself, wasn't always the shining beacon of wholesomeness she suggested in her writing. She was feisty, retaliatory, and sometimes even a little conniving! Although, that only serves to make me love her more, to be honest!

There are only two places in the *Little House* series where we know for sure that Laura deliberately changed the names of characters to protect their identity. She was, after all, writing some very uncomfortable things about them! One was Nellie, of course. The other name change was for the Brewsters, with whom she boarded during her first term as a school teacher. Their real name was Bouchie, and the whole family was probably quite thankful that the image of a maniacally depressed, knife-wielding woman wasn't eternally linked to that name. (Unfortunately for them, between the fervor of rabid *Little House* researchers and the advent of the Internet, it is, now!)

The character of Nellie Oleson, however, was not just a name change to protect an unpleasant identity. It was also an umbrella under which three different people were brought together: Nellie Owens, Genevieve Masters, and Estella Gilbert.

Laura would have no idea when she first wrote "Little House in the Big Woods" what success would follow, nor the large number of books she'd end up writing. So, when she first introduced Nellie to us in "On the Banks of Plum Creek," it was Nellie Owens whom she was referring to, and it was her that the fictional character was obviously named after.

Later, when Genevieve Masters showed up in Walnut Grove, and proved to be as much of a thorn in Laura's side as Nellie Owens was, their characters began to mingle. The Ingalls family didn't stay long in Minnesota, however; they moved to De Smet, South Dakota, just a few years later. Much to Laura's chagrin, Gennie's family showed up there, too. At least Nellie Owens didn't arrive, as well!

Instead of creating a whole new nemesis in her now blossoming series, Laura decided to bring the fictitious Ms. Oleson out west, and ascribe Gennie's antics (as well as Laura's intense dislike of her) to the character of Nellie. Not only did it conceal Genevieve's real identity, it also simplified the story and continued the brilliantly devised character of Nellie, who had already acquired a surprising following. It's important to note that, although feisty when young, the mature Laura had no desire to publicly harm anyone, even if they had done her wrong in real life. So, the decision to obscure Gennie's misdeeds behind the character of Nellie Oleson was probably as much about not maligning her character as it was to continue the narrative flow of Nellie's story.

Of the three women Laura used as models for Nellie, Estella Gilbert played the least significant role. Neither her name, general character, nor appearance seems to be incorporated into the composite, but she was still an important addition. Her story added delicious tension and richness to the budding romance of Almanzo and Laura toward the end of the series. Laura didn't like her much, either, but with nowhere near the animosity she felt toward the other Nellies.

In researching Nellie Owens, Genevieve Masters, and Estella Gilbert, one thing became abundantly clear: each of these women is fascinating in her own right, and their stories are more compelling than the fictional character of Nellie Oleson could ever suggest. I hope after meeting them, you'll feel the same way, too.

NELLIE
OWENS

NELLIE WINIFRED OWENS

Born August 2nd, 1868, near LeRoy, Mower County, Minnesota
Died November 2nd, 1949, in Portland, Multnomah County, Oregon

Nellie Owens is the "Nellie" most has been written about. For a number of years, when Laura Ingalls Wilder first began publishing her *Little House* books, readers thought she was the *only* Nellie Oleson, and that Laura Ingalls Wilder had simply modified her last name to protect the Owens family from embarrassment. But as Laura's fame, and interest in the Nellie character grew, fans and researchers began to realize that Nellie had to be either part fiction or some sort of composite character. Since Nellie Owens never lived in De Smet, and her only interaction with Laura was in Walnut Grove, the fact that Nellie Oleson appears in "Little Town on the Prairie" and "These Happy Golden Years" was a little confusing. Thankfully, Laura's original manuscripts, writing notes, and letters to her daughter, Rose Wilder Lane, emerged. From these treasures, riveted fans learned the truth. . .Nellie Owens was only one of three young women who made up the character.

The part Nellie Owens plays in the character's development is crucial, however. Her persona sets the tone for Nellie Oleson's future demeanor and establishes the delicious rivalry that Laura chronicles throughout the series. The real Nellie and Laura are pretty young when their enmity begins. "On the Banks of Plum Creek" describes their first meeting in the school yard where Nellie looks down her nose at newly arrived Mary and Laura, and pronounces them merely "country girls." In that scene, Laura is supposed to be "almost eight years old." As Nellie Owens was a year and a half younger than Laura, she would have been approximately six and a half. That's awfully young to be so snooty and classist. And her brother, Willie, who was with her in that scene, would have been only five!

In real life, Laura's family lived in Walnut Grove twice, once between 1874-1876, and again between 1878-1879. In "Pioneer Girl[1]," Laura writes about her interactions with Nellie as being in that earlier timeframe. So Laura would have been between seven and nine, and Nellie would have been between six and eight when the bulk of their conflict occurred.

As they were such young children, their initial skirmishes developed around childish things. In "On the Banks of Plum Creek," Laura devotes two consecutive chapters to the pettiness of Nellie, recounting her insistence on dominating schoolyard games:

> The little girls always played ring-around-a-rosy, because Nellie Oleson said to. They got tired of it, but they always played it, until one day, before Nellie could say anything, Laura said, "Let's play Uncle John!"

> "Let's! Let's! the girls said, taking hold of hands. But Nellie grabbed both hands full of Laura's long hair and jerked her flat on the ground.

> "No! No!" Nellie shouted. "I want to play ring-around-a-rosy!"

> Laura jumped up and her hand flashed out to slap Nellie. She stopped just in time. Pa said she must never strike anybody.

And then, Laura outlines Nellie's selfishness with her and Willie's toys:

> Nellie and Willie had toys—tops and jumping jacks and picture books. It was a great treat to see such toys, though Nellie and Willie never let us play with them. . .

> Nellie had a most wonderful doll which she kept wrapped in soft paper and laid in a box. This doll had a china head, with

---

[1] All references to "Pioneer Girl" are to *Pioneer Girl: The Annotated Autobiography*, edited by Pamela Smith Hill, unless otherwise noted.

black china hair; her cheeks and mouth were red and long eye-lashes were painted around her blue eyes. . .We did want so much just to touch her, even only once. I would have given anything to hold her in my arms. (Lawson, *Pioneer Girl* unpub. manuscript)

Of course, Laura wasn't exactly an angel, either. She really did retaliate against Nellie's frequent selfishness, and her impudence to Ma, by luring her into a leech-infested part of the creek. This story made it into "On the Banks of Plum Creek" almost exactly as it really happened. In "Pioneer Girl," Laura confesses:

When Nellie and Willie came from town to play with us, I would lead them near the old crab's stone, and when he chased them they would run screaming into the bloodsucker's pool. The slimy bloodsuckers would fasten on their feet and legs.

At first they tried to brush them off. Then they kicked and danced and screeched, while I rolled on the grass and laughed.

Nellie and Willie never suspected that I lured them that way on purpose, and they never learned to beware of the old crab before he chased them. (*Ibid.*)

The "On the Banks of Plum Creek" version of the incident was almost identical, though this time, Willie wasn't there. As Laura mentions at the end of the previous quote, this trick was played on Nellie, and sometimes Willie, a number of times, and yet they never caught on. The fictional version is set in the country party scene:

[Laura] led the girls wading near the old crab's home. The noise and the splashing had driven him under his rock. She saw his angry claws and his browny-green head peeping out, and she crowded Nellie near him. Then she kicked a big splash of water onto his rock and she screamed, "Ooh, Nellie! Nellie, look out!"

. . .Nellie ran screaming straight into the muddy water under the plum thicket.

Nellie came out into the clean water. She tried to wash her muddy skirt and then she tried to wash her feet, and then she screamed.

Muddy brown bloodsuckers were sticking to her legs and her feet.

She couldn't wash them off. She tried to pick one off, then she ran screaming up the creek bank. There she stood kicking as hard as she could, first one foot and then the other, screaming all the time.

Laura laughed till she fell on the grass and rolled. "Oh, look, look!" She shouted, laughing. "See Nellie dance!"

A more mature and introspective Laura later wrote that she was sure Nellie "was much more unhappy than she ever could have made me." Given she used the name "Nellie" rather than Genevieve or Estella, it's assumed she was speaking of Nellie Owens. And that's an astute observation: people rarely bully others unless they, themselves, are unhappy. Though we have few real clues as to why Nellie Owens might have been unhappy, Laura guessed that Nellie's mother might have contributed to the issue. From "Pioneer Girl:"

> [Nellie] and Willie would help themselves to candy out of the store and eat it before us never offering us any.

> We would not have been allowed to be so rude and selfish but Mrs Owen never seemed to care.

And

> . . .at that time we did not know that children would ever diso-
> bey their mothers, so we thought that Mrs. Owen did not care.

Things got a little more challenging for Nellie Owens when
Genevieve Masters arrived in Walnut Grove in 1878. This was after the Ingalls moved back to Walnut Grove the second time. Laura
would have been about eleven, Nellie would have been ten, and
Genevieve around eleven, as well. As soon as Gennie arrived in
town, she attempted to usurp Nellie Owens' role as leader of the
girls. Laura described their conflict in "Pioneer Girl:"

> Nellie was still a leader among the girls when Genieve[2] came
> and did not intend to give up her leadership. She tried to hold it
> by being free with candy and bits of ribbon from her father's
> store.

It must have been a challenging rivalry between two strong-
willed, bossy girls, especially since Genevieve's father taught the
town's school at some point during the Masters' time in Walnut
Grove. And there must have been some blending of Nellie Owens
and Genevieve Masters into the character of Nellie Oleson. In a
letter to her daughter, Rose Wilder Lane, dated March 15th, 1938,
Laura says that she thinks she "will let Nellie Oleson take Jennie
Masters' place in Prairie Girl[3] and let her be the only girl from
Plum Creek. Their characters were alike."

So it was an easy choice to let the character of Nellie Oleson,
so beautifully grounded by the persona and behavior of Nellie

---

[2] Laura referred to Genevieve Masters as "Genieve" throughout *Pioneer Girl*.

[3] *Prairie Girl* was later split into "Little Town on the Prairie" and "These Happy
Golden Years."

Owens, be the umbrella under which Gennie, and eventually Estella Gilbert, would come.

The Ingalls family left Walnut Grove in 1879, when Laura was twelve years old and Nellie Owens was about ten or eleven years old. It is presumed that Laura and Nellie Owens never saw each other again.

Early Life

Nellie Owens was born on August 2nd, 1868, in LeRoy, Mower County, Minnesota, and was the first born of William Henry Owens and Margaret H. Gibson. William is generally believed to have been born in Pennsylvania. However, we've found only one historical document, the 1920 Federal Census, which supports this conclusion. Every other source, including multiple censuses, and all circumstantial evidence, indicates New York as his actual place of birth. William's wife, Margaret, was born in Canada, less than four miles from the American border, and, coincidentally, less than thirty miles north of Almanzo Wilder's boyhood home in Malone, New York.

Where William and Margaret were married is also up for debate. A *LORE* article, Volume 23, Issue 2, (published in the fall/winter edition of 1997/98), citing information gleaned from several descendants of William, gives Cresco, Iowa, and March 20th, 1864, as William and Margaret's marriage details. However, this is the only reference we can find to that location and date; there are no other historical documents supporting this information. There are several that contradict it, however. A New York State Census in 1865, just a year after William and Margaret were supposed to have been wed, for example, lists William as living with his parents in Utica, New York, and no wife is with him. Later, in the 1900 Federal Census, William reports himself as having been married for thirty-four years. That would have made his marriage year somewhere between 1865 and 1866, which also contradicts the Cresco date. So, it's highly unlikely that either the place or year are correct.

In the 1870 Federal Census, however, William and Margaret are married, living in Beaver Township, Fillmore County, Minnesota, and had Nellie, who was two, and Willie, who was one, with them. Assuming they did marriage and child-bearing in the traditional order, this would mean they had to have been wed sometime between June of 1865 (when the New York State Census was taken) and November of 1867 (the earliest conception month for Nellie). This, of course, corroborates William's claim of being married around 1866-7 on the 1900 census. But that is still a pretty eventful few years, isn't it? Living in New York in 1865, married in about 1866, moved over a thousand miles west by 1868, and a father of two by 1869!

In Beaver Township, William is farming, with healthy assets: $3,500.00 worth of real estate and a personal estate worth $1,500.00. In 1873, William moved the family again, this time about two hundred and forty miles southwest to North Hero Township, in Redwood County, Minnesota. Their property in North Hero was very close to the Ingalls' farm and in the greater Walnut Grove area. Though farming, too, it looks like William opened his first store in 1875. By 1880, the Owens had moved into Walnut Grove proper, and was listed on the census as working in "General Merchandise." Eleven year old Nellie and ten year old Willie were listed as "at school." Despite the census nod to William, the store was primarily managed by Margaret, while William engaged in a number of enterprises on the side: he farmed, bought and sold stock, and practiced veterinary medicine, something he learned back on his parent's thriving New York farmstead.

In 1882, neighbor Lafayette Bedal died tragically in a lumber mill accident. Though Laura later wrote of a "Miss Beadle" as a teacher, Lafayette's daughter, Eva, couldn't have been who she was referring to. . .she was hardly more than a toddler when Laura went to school in Walnut Grove. We have more details from a biography on Lafayette:

> Lafayette kept a grocery store and opened the first school in his home in the winter of 1873-1874 with 15 pupils. He also taught a Sunday school class in his home. Lafayette (or perhaps his fa-

ther Elias) is the "Mr. Beadle" mentioned in Laura Ingalls Wilder book "On the Banks of Plum Creek." It is not clear who the teacher "Miss Eva Beadle" actually was, since the only Eva in the family at that time was Lafayette's three-year-old daughter. It is possible that the teacher was Clementia Bedal, but more likely Lafayette himself was the teacher. (Bedal, Sheryl J.)

After his very premature death, Lafayette's wife, Clementia, was left to care for their nine children, but could not do it alone. To help, several of her children were taken in by friends and neighbors, and her five-year-old son, Frank, was one of those. He went to live with the Owens as a companion for their partially-sighted son, Willie.

Despite seeming to prosper in Walnut Grove, the pioneering family decided to head west again, this time all the way to the west coast. Some descendants have speculated that the Owens might have traveled in a wagon along the famous Oregon Trail. There are a couple of solid reasons why that is not the likeliest option, however. Some sources believe the family started their westward journey in 1883, but William sold his mercantile to Frank H. Smith in January of 1884, so that's a far likelier start date. And if that is a correct sale date, the family probably waited until after the store was sold to start their journey.

Daniel D. Peterson, in his book "What Happened to Those People" states that the family settled in beautiful Ferndale, Humboldt County, California, and joined the Adventist church there, in February 1884. The distance between Walnut Grove, Minnesota, and Ferndale, California, is almost two thousand miles, and the Oregon Trail ends about thirteen miles south of Portland, not in Northern California. That's way too much ground to cover in a wagon in about a month, even if it wasn't the middle of winter, which it was. Also, the Owens had decent assets listed on the 1870 census, and seemed to continue prospering in the ensuing years via a number of profitable enterprises. For example, the Redwood Falls Gazette published an interesting tidbit in their January 23rd, 1879, edition:

> W.H. Owens has put up about fifteen ton of ice for family use next summer. (Peterson, 2013)

A man of even modest means, who'd just sold his home, farm, and business, and had the discretionary income to put up "about fifteen tons of ice for family use" in summer, would likely have traveled those two thousand miles via the quickest and most comfortable method. It's romantic to think of them on the Oregon Trail, but it's far more likely that the Owens came west by train.

In Ferndale, a lush Victorian dairy community along the north coast of California, William established himself again in many trades: a farmer, a veterinarian, a real estate investor, a farrier, and a blacksmith. As if that wasn't enough, in 1889, he opened another successful mercantile, which he operated until he moved the family to Tillamook, Oregon, in 1891.

It was shortly after arriving in Ferndale in 1884 that Nellie, who would have been about fifteen years old, met her future husband, Henry Kirry, though they wouldn't marry until nine years later.

After approximately seven years in Ferndale, Nellie moved with her family to Tillamook County, Oregon, where she taught school from around 1891 to 1893 before marrying Henry in 1893.

Married Life and Death

The Owens and the Kirry families became friends through the Adventist Church in Ferndale very shortly after the Owens joined in February of 1884. The 1880 census lists Mrs. Josephine Kirry and many of her children as living in Ferndale, but her husband, and Henry's father, Oswald Kirry, was not with them, though he was still living. Henry Francis (though some sources mistakenly list Franklin as his middle name) Kirry was the seventh of Josephine and Oswald's nine children. He was born on March 20th, 1869, in Philo, a small town in Mendocino County, California.

Henry would have been only fourteen, or newly fifteen, when he first met Nellie. It's unlikely that they had any romantic notions that young, but even if theirs was a "love-at-first-sight" situation, circumstances would make courting difficult. In an article in "The Best of the LORE," their problem is described:

> Henry's older brother, Walter, about this time offered Henry a job along with him hauling logs on a tug from Mendocino Bay to [San] Francisco. So Henry was often away from Ferndale, making it difficult at times to pursue his budding relationship with Nellie.

Henry worked with his brother for years on different boats, traveling up and down the coast of California and Oregon, though he still considered Humboldt County, California, his home base. In 1890, Henry had signed a Voter Registration form in his town of residence, Eureka, California, which is Humboldt's county seat and is just north of Ferndale. He was twenty-one at the time and had left the boats behind, having changed careers by becoming a blacksmith.

By the next year, 1891, Henry had moved again, establishing a successful blacksmith's shop in Bay City, Oregon. The "Statesman Journal" from Salem, Oregon, notes that by May 28th, 1891, "H.F.

Kirry has got his blacksmith shop running in good shape. He is a first-class workman and is turning out some good work."

Given the Owens move from Ferndale, California, to Tillamook County, Oregon, in that same year, this appears to be approximately when Henry and Nellie began to get serious. Henry is no longer sailing up and down the pacific coast and has moved very close to Nellie. Nellie, meanwhile, has taken up a new profession, too: she is working as a schoolteacher in Tillamook:

> Nellie was now a teacher at a small schoolhouse in the area where she taught students reading, writing, orthography [spelling!], mental and written arithmetic, geography, history, physiology, and civil government. (Waskin)

Two years after the couple moved (separately) to Oregon, they married in Tillamook in July of 1893, on either the 24th or the 26th. Just a year later, in 1894, they welcomed their first daughter, Zola. In 1896, son Lloyd arrived. Their last child, son Leslie Henry, made his appearance in 1900. All of Nellie and Henry's children were born in Bay City, Tillamook County, Oregon.

Curiously, on January 7th, 1898, a homesteading land patent was issued to Nellie in Tillamook County for one hundred and sixty acres. Her brother, Willie, also had a homesteading land patent issued in the same township four months later, on May 2nd. This is interesting, and a little dodgy, for several reasons. One is that the patent was issued to Nellie, not Henry. In order for the patent to be in her name, instead of his, she had to have applied for the homestead before they were married. According to the Bureau of Land Management, for a woman to be granted a land patent, the following conditions had to apply:

> Even before they had the right to vote, women over age 21 who were heads of their households were able to receive homestead

patents. This included widows, those with disabled husbands, and single women. (BLM, *Shaping America's History*)

So, for it to be in her name, she had to have been the head of her own household. As she was obviously not a widow, hadn't yet been married, nor was Henry disabled any time in their early marriage, the only way she could have qualified for a homestead was as a single woman. And, of course, the only time she was single was before July of 1893, when she married Henry. Since she was teaching in 1892 and 1893, and she was in her mid-twenties, it was entirely probable that she was living on her own, or at least claiming she was. And, if she was, indeed, living on her own, and not secretly with her parents or brother, she would have legally qualified to apply for a free (except for filing fees) one-hundred-and-sixty-acre homestead.

And the timing certainly fits. If she received her patent in January of 1898, that would mean she first applied in late 1892 or very early January of 1893. Why? Because, under the Homestead Act of 1862, it took five years to "prove up" on a claim. The requirements for "proving up" were fairly simple: a homestead had to be lived on by the applicant for five years, a dwelling at least twelve by fourteen feet had to be constructed, the land had to be "improved," and the homestead needed to produce crops. If those few conditions were met, the applicant would qualify to receive their "free land" via a homesteading land patent.

The dodgy bit of Nellie's equation comes with the stipulation that the land be "lived on" by the applicant. In Nellie's case, it's pretty clear that she didn't, actually, live on the property. At least not for long if she ever did. Nellie and Henry married less than a year after Nellie must have applied for the claim. But every indication is that Nellie and Henry made their home in Bay City, not on the homestead:

- Henry's blacksmith shop was in Bay City.
- All of their children, starting just a year into their marriage, were born in Bay City.
- Bay City is right on the coast and a full twelve miles north of her homestead, a distance too far to commute to work at that time.
- Two of their children were born during the years she would have been legally required to be living on the claim (Zola, in 1894 and Lloyd, in 1896).
- And, of course, neither Henry nor Nellie were farmers.

Willie's own claim was very near Nellie's, though, so it's possible that he farmed it for her while she lived with Henry and her kids in town. Or perhaps it was her father or a hired man. And of course, it's possible the land was never improved or farmed at all. However the situation played out, it almost certainly wasn't legal. Nellie might have applied with honest intentions, but it looks like she didn't fulfill the homesteading requirements legitimately.

To be fair, there was a stipulation in the Homestead Act that an applicant could pay $1.25 per acre, with far less stringent "improvements" required, after six months. But if that was the route she took, she would not have received a patent in her name five years after she was no longer a single woman. Although a possibility, it looks highly unlikely.

Interestingly, just two years after Nellie received her land patent, the 1900 census lists the Kirry's as still living in Bay City, with Henry continuing his work as a blacksmith. But they are living in a house (specifically not a farm) that they own outright. That's a pretty decent accomplishment for a young couple from modest means not many years into their marriage. Don't you think?

However they acquired their properties, and however well set up financially they seemed to be so quickly, things in the Kirry household started to disintegrate. By 1907, Henry was back working on boats, this time as an engineer on the steamer "No Wonder," which sailed out of Portland. The family moved to Forest Grove, Oregon, which is about sixty miles due east of Bay City, and much closer to Portland, around this time. We don't know exactly when, but it would make sense if it correlated with the start date for Henry's new engineering job. This new position meant that Henry spent a great deal of time away from home.

Skip Buhler, a researcher for the "Friends of Historic Forest Grove" noted that the Kirry's last known home in Forest Grove "was built in 1912, but again they owned the land as early as 1909, and likely did for some years before." The house, which still stands, was listed as a "farm," but it would have been a very small one as it was only on about five acres. Of course, Henry was not home enough to work a significant plot of land, anyway, even if he had been so inclined. So it was probably more of a smallholding, used mostly to grow food for the family.

Why did they choose Forest Grove? Nellie believed the beautiful little town was a better environment for their children to be raised in. Plus, it was much closer to Henry's work out of Portland. Given their eventual split, I think it might have been Nellie's final bid to save their marriage.

The family were still in Forest Grove on the 1920 census, and Henry is still working as a "Marine Engineer." But at some time during that year, Nellie and Henry's marriage finally broke down and they officially separated. By 1921, Nellie is living with her daughter, Zola, in Portland. Their divorce wasn't official until November 15th, 1925, however. It was granted in Washington County, where Forest Grove is located. As the divorce decree wasn't finalized until four years after Nellie had moved to Portland, it's assumed that Henry remained, at least until formally filing for divorce, in Forest Grove.

Curiously, Nellie lists herself as widowed in a 1928 City Directory for Portland, though Henry is very much alive for more than another twenty years. This is something that her former mother-in-law, Josephine Kirry, did as well—listing herself on multiple official documents as "widowed" when her husband was still alive. Her husband, Oswald, lists himself as divorced on the 1900 census, but Josephine never did.

Henry, however, on a United States Merchant Seamen Census in 1930, has no problem disclosing his true marital status: he is listed as divorced. He's living in Astoria, which is at the mouth of the Columbia River, northwest of Portland. He's sixty, but still working on a steamer.

Nellie has taken a room in the home of Mr. and Mrs. Galen Whitcomb by 1930. She lists her job as "no occupation" and again incorrectly describes herself as widowed. She would have been about sixty-two. By 1931 she's living with Zola again, and they're roommates for at least three years, living in two different apartments together. We couldn't locate the Portland City Directories from 1935-1937, but in the 1938 edition, Nellie is strangely not listed, and we can't find her elsewhere.

Between 1939 and 1944, however, she's living in Portland at the Patton Home for the Aged and still erroneously listed as widowed. Not long after her eighty-first birthday, Nellie's health began to decline. She was transferred to another Portland facility, but didn't improve. In late October, she contracted pneumonia, and died a week later on November 2nd, 1949. She is buried near her father and brother in the Forest View Cemetery in Forest Grove. Her funeral notice was posted in The Oregonian on November 4th, 1949:

KIRRY - Nellie W., Nov. 2, 8610 NE Beech; mother of Mrs. Reginald Sheard, Lloyd Kirry; grandmother of Robert and Prescott Kirry; 4 great-grandchildren. Service Saturday, 9:30 am, at The House of Holman, Hawthorne at 27th. Friends invited. Interment Forest View Cemetery, Forest Grove, at 11 am. (FindAGrave)

After moving back to Tillamook in 1935, Henry also eventually found his way to Portland, possibly to be nearer his children, where he died almost exactly two years after Nellie, on November 17th, 1951. He is buried in the River View Cemetery in Portland.

Family

Children

Henry and Nellie had three children: Zola Margaret Kirry was born on the August 1st, 1894, Lloyd Prescott Kirry was born on July 12th, 1896, and Leslie Henry Kirry was born on April 1st, 1900. All of the Kirry children were born in Bay City, Oregon.

Zola Margaret Kirry Sheard (1894 – 1986)

By all indications, Zola and Nellie were very close. After Nellie and Henry separated, Zola and Nellie lived together for many years in multiple locations in Portland, and visited each other often when they weren't. Zola attended the University of Oregon Normal School, which is now called Western Oregon University, between 1917 and 1922. Like her mom, Zola became a school teacher, working in and around the Portland area, as well as Eugene, Oregon, for about forty years. Zola and her brother, Lloyd, were close, too, and also shared apartments, or lived very close-by each other.

Zola married fairly late in life, some time between 1938 and 1940, when she would have been well into her forties. Her husband, Reginald Sheard, was born on March 5th, 1897, in Cape Town, South Africa, to British parents. Reginald was educated in Canada, where he also served in the Canadian military. After one military engagement, he was awarded the Military Medal for bravery. In 1924, at the age of twenty-seven, Reginald applied for naturalization in the U.S., when he was married to his first wife, Olive.

By the time of the 1940 census, Zola and Reginald were financially comfortable. She was working as a public school teacher and Reginald was working at the Federal Reserve Bank. Their rented accommodation cost them only $33.00 per month, but their combined income was about $4,500.00 per year, or about $375.00

per month. Though not rich, they were very solidly in the middle class.

Reginald died on November 20th, 1983. Zola died a few years later, on September 28th, 1986, in Portland. Zola was cremated and her ashes were scattered at sea.

Lloyd Prescott Kirry (1896 – 1961)

Henry and Nellie's second child, Lloyd, was born on July 12th, 1896. By all accounts, Lloyd's life was a mix of significant highs and some dramatic lows. He started out well, though. There's a brilliant picture of Lloyd and his Forest Grove High School football team available in Google Books in which he's the only one wearing a helmet. He played for his school in 1914-1915 when he would have been eighteen or nineteen.

In 1920, on June 24th, Lloyd married Barbara Jean Buchanan (born c.1901) in a fairytale wedding at the home of her parents, Mr. and Mrs. John C. Buchanan:

KIRRY-BUCHANAN

One of the most elaborate and delightfully charming weddings in Forest Grove's recent social history occurred on Thursday evening of last week at the beautiful home of Mr. and Mrs. John C. Buchanan in South Park when their eldest daughter, Miss Barbara Jean, became the bride of Mr. Lloyd Prescott Kirry, son of Mr. and Mrs. H. F. Kirry, of this city. —Forest Grove News-Times (*Beaverton Times*, July 2, 1920)

Shortly thereafter, in 1921, Lloyd began a very long career with the Standard Oil Company, mostly in sales. It's unclear where Lloyd and Barbara first made their home together, but by 1926, they were living in Portland and in 1927, their only child, son Lloyd Prescott Jr., was born. They continued living in Portland, often close to Nellie, through the end of the 1920's.

In 1931, the couple were briefly living in Walla Walla, Washington, but were back in Portland, this time sharing an address with Lloyd's older sister, Zola by 1933. And this is where things seem to come apart a bit. Barbara is no long being listed with him in city directories by 1934. Sometime in the mid to late 1930's, they divorced. In July of 1937, however, Lloyd must have hit rock bottom and he was arrested for drunkenness, though his behavior seemed a little more suicidal than just inebriated:

POLICE SAVE THEN ARREST SALESMAN

Portland, July 24 AP-Firemen and harbor policemen first saved Lloyd P. Kirry, 40, a salesmen, from the burning deck of a boat and then arrested him on charges of drunkenness.

Policeman G. A. Patterson said Kirry jumped aboard a 41-foot launch after the captain and four passengers had abandoned it when a gasoline explosion set it afire.

From the burning hull, Kirry served notice that he was claiming salvage rights and refused to heed commands of firemen to get off, Finally firemen lassoed him and pulled him off, after which police arrested him. The launch was destroyed with an estimated loss of S2,500. (*Daily Capital Journal*, July 24, 1937)

Thankfully, Lloyd seemed to pull things together and, by 1940, he was married again. Gladys E. Olson, born in 1912, was fifteen and a half years his junior. In 1951, Lloyd was awarded a gold pin for thirty years of service with Standard Oil. It's likely that Gladys and Lloyd divorced, too, possibly around 1959. We found a divorce record for a Gladys E. Kirry, born in 1912, in Portland, but in Lloyd's obituary, two years later, she's still listed as his wife.

Lloyd died in Eugene, Oregon, on October 12th, 1961, at sixty-five years of age:

Obituary of Lloyd P. Kirry

KIRRY—Lloyd Prescott Kirry of 1782 Alder, passed away Thursday, October 12, 1961. He was born July 12, 1896 at Bay City, Oregon. He had been a sales engineer with Standard Oil Company in Portland and Eugene, retiring in August 1961 after 40 years service, He was a member of the Holbrook Masonic Lodge #30 at Forrest [sic] Grove and the Marine Engineers Beneficial Association. He is survived by his wife, Gladys; a son, Lloyd Prescott Kirry Jr. of Olympia, Washington; 7 grandchildren; a sister, Zola Kirry Sheard of Portland. Funeral services will be held Monday, October 16, 1961 at 2 p.m., in the England Funeral Home, Pearl at 18th, Reverend Steen Whiteside officiating.

Entombment in Rest Haven Mausoleum. (*Eugene Guard*, Oct 13th, 1961)

Leslie Henry ("Duff") Kirry (1900 – 1931)

The last Kirry child was Leslie Henry, who went by the nickname "Duff." Like his older siblings, Duff was born in Bay City, and he entered the world on April 1st, 1900. And his life was even more tragic than his older brother's.

Things started out well, however. In 1920, he attended the University of Washington, but didn't seem to finish his education. On November 16th, 1921, he married Agnes Lucile Galt (June 1st, 1901-April 12th, 1984):

Kirry-Galt

One of the prettiest weddings of the season occurred Wednesday, Nov. 16th, 1921, when Miss Agnes Lucile Galt, only daughter of Mr. and Mrs. H. H. Galt, was united in marriage to Leslie Henry Kirry, son of Mr. and Mrs. H. F. Kirry, of Portland, former residents of this city, at the home of the bride's parents on Greenville Road, at 4:30 in the afternoon.

The Rev. W. Walter Blair performed a most beautiful, yet simple ceremony.

The bride entered the room on the arm of her father, carrying a huge boquet [sic] of May Martin roses. Miss Lucile Robinson, carrying a beautiful boquet of Ophelia roses, acted as bridesmaid and Martin Enschede as best man. The shower boquet was Vovordia.

The home was tastily decorated with yellow chrisanthemums [sic] and lighted yellow candles also ornamented the rooms. After congratulations the guests were invited to the dining room where the bride's cake was cut by the bride, and refreshments of ice cream, cake and coffee were served by four of her campfire girl friends, Misses Clara and Agnes Fenenga, Ruth Burlingham and Mabel Patton. Mrs. W. J McCready cut the ices, Mrs. L. P. Rockwood poured, and Mesdames W. G. Harrington and M. R. Johnson assisted about the rooms.

Russell Beals presided at the piano.

Many beautiful and useful gifts were received.

They left by auto early in the evening, taking the train at Hillsboro, for Seattle, where the groom is in business and where they will make their future home.

Many friends join in congratulations to this happy couple who were very popular among the younger set, both being graduates of our local High School and being residents of this city for a number of years. Mr. Kirry last year attended the University of Washington. (*Beaverton Times*, Nov 18, 1921)

The following year, their only child, Robert Henry Kirry, was born in King County, Washington, on September 10th, 1922. From 1925 through 1931, Duff was listed on every City Directory for Seattle as a "meat cutter," which is a butcher. Unfortunately, at just a month shy of his thirty-first birthday, Duff died in Seattle on March 2nd, 1931. He's buried in Acacia Memorial Park in King County, Washington.

Agnes stayed on in Seattle, and was the District Supervisor for Ballard Branch Family Society of Seattle by 1942. In that year, their son, who became an airline pilot, married Lorismae Hogwood in Yuma, Arizona. Tragically, Robert died prematurely, too, at just thirty-five, on March 17th, 1958, while on a fishing trip in Puget Sound. Agnes died in March of 1984.

Grandparents

Nellie's paternal grandparents were **Robert H. Owens** (born approximately 1804) and **Winifred R. Evans** (born approximately 1810). Both Robert and Winifred were from Wales, but their exact birth and death dates are unknown.

Nellie's maternal, "**Gibson**" grandparents are a mystery. Our research indicates that accepted facts (such as where and when William and Margaret married) are incorrect. Census information lists several possible places of birth for the two, including Scotland, Ireland, and Canada. Initial research suggests Scotland as the birthplace of Margaret's father, and Canada for her mother. We're starting to tease out more clues, however, and intend to track Nellie's maternal grandparents down!

Parents

Though it appears most researchers believe that Nellie's father, **William Henry Owens**, was born in 1836 in Scranton, Pennsylvania, *every* census in which he appears (except the 1920 version, which was taken after he's been admitted to an insane asylum) indicates he was born in New York state. The 1865 New York State census lists the applicant's specific place of birth on its form, and Oneida, NY, is marked for William.

Interestingly, though all but the last census cites New York as his birthplace, historical documents don't seem to agree on his birth year. Several dates, ranging from 1836 to 1841, are offered as possibilities. Some are calculated from William's stated age at the time the individual censuses are taken, but the 1900 census expressly states a birth month and year of July 1838. The 1888 Humboldt County Voter Registrations seems to confirm this year, indicating he was born 1838/9 in New York. So, it seems confirmed that William was born in New York, and that his likeliest birth year was 1838.

Why are many researchers wrong, then? Possibly because they gleaned their information from the last census taken before William's death. The 1920 Census lists a widowed W. H. Owens living as an inmate in the Oregon State Insane Asylum [which is now called the Oregon State Hospital], in Salem, Marion County, Oregon. He's recorded as being eighty-three years old, with a birth year of 1836, and having been born in Pennsylvania to parents born in Wales. The problem is that this one census contradicts every other census ever taken, and we don't know how this information was obtained. It could have been from an ill-informed hospital staff member. If it was from William, himself, which is unlikely considering where he was, he was well past being a reliable source of even his own historical information. Being an inmate in an asylum could indicate that he was insane, or perhaps suffering from severe dementia or something similar. Therefore, he's not the most credible of sources at this point.

When he was young, however, William's folks were successful farmers in New York state, and that's where he learned both farming and veterinary medicine, two professions he later practiced. In May of 1875, he opened his Walnut Grove general store, which he ran until he sold it to Frank H. Smith in 1884. He was also a veterinarian on the side, and bought and sold stock (cattle, etc., not shares in businesses!). In 1879, at the first meeting of the Walnut Grove village council, he was elected town treasurer, so he was clearly viewed as a successful businessman. Pa Ingalls was elected as a justice of the peace at the same meeting.

In 1883, as a member of the School Board, William was appointed along with Elias Bedal and Frederick F. Goff to find an appropriate location for a new, bigger school. By January of 1884, however, he had sold the mercantile and was headed away from the prairie.

His destination was the west coast and he ended up in the gorgeous coastal village of Ferndale, Humboldt County, California. Ferndale was a prolific center of dairy farming, nestled between the giant coastal redwood forests and the Pacific Ocean. Unlike the dry and variable prairies, Humboldt County's climate offered reliable rainfall to irrigate the lush pasturelands which defined the area. Perfect for raising dairy cows.

Just after arriving, William and his family joined the Adventist church in February of 1884. He returned to farming, assimilating himself into the local dairy industry, and he also invested in real estate and worked as a blacksmith. He even opened another successful general store in 1889, which he ran profitably for two years.

But in 1891, he moved the family again. This time, it was further north to Tillamook County, Oregon, another celebrated center of dairy farming. Tillamook was then, and still is, particularly famous for its cheese. He continued to farm in his new home, and also returned to veterinary medicine.

By the time of his death, on November 17th, 1920, he was a widowed "inmate" in the Oregon State Insane Asylum in Salem, Oregon. From all accounts, it was a pretty unsavory place, and it was even the location for the filming of the movie "One Flew Over the Cuckoo's Nest."

Terwilliger Funeral Home Records cite the cause of death as organ and heart disease, which other sources state was simply a heart attack. It's not confirmed that William was literally insane, however. Places such as this asylum were often "catch-all" facilities for people with a variety of conditions that had nowhere else to go. Inmates could have dementia, brain damage, severe depression, or a number of other issues. Because of the variety of conditions, some of which were misdiagnosed or misunderstood a hundred years ago, "hospitals" like this one often did little more than keep its inmates alive. It was a sad end to what, by all accounts, was a happy and productive life.

William is buried in Forest View Cemetery, in Forest Grove, where Nellie and Willie are also buried.

Nellie's mother, **Margaret H. Gibson**, was born in Huntingdon, Hinchinbrooke, Quebec, on January 12th, 1836. Though in Canada, Hinchinbrooke was only four miles from the U.S. border and, coincidentally, just thirty miles north of Almanzo Wilder's family farm in Malone, New York. Margaret's parents have been listed as being born in Scotland, Ireland, or Canada, so it's unclear exactly where they're from. But Margaret emigrated to the U.S. in 1848 and married William Owens in about 1866. Nellie was born in 1868 and Willie was born just over a year later, in 1869.

Much like her television counterpart, Margaret was primarily responsible for running both the family home and the mercantiles they owned while William was farming, doing his veterinary work, or traveling to buy and sell stock.

While living in Walnut Grove, Margaret suffered multiple attacks of diphtheria, which is the same illness both Laura and Almanzo contracted later in De Smet, and which caused Almanzo to suffer a stroke. Almanzo never quite regained full health or full sensation in his leg after his illness. Diphtheria wasn't uncommon in the area, either; it was a serious epidemic in Walnut Grove, and reached its pinnacle in 1879-1880. Several locals died from the disease:

> In 1879 and 1880 a diphtheria epidemic hit the area. ... "All persons who have in any way been exposed to the Small Pox are hereby notified not to enter the corporate limits of the village of Walnut Grove until permition (sic) is given by the Council. Any person violating such order will be punished as prescribed by law." (Peterson, 2014)

Thankfully, though contracting the disease more than once, Margaret survived.

Though later a staunch Adventist on the west coast, Margaret was a charter member of the Congregationalist Church while in Walnut Grove. Interestingly, William was not. It was typical for couples to pursue such church-related activities together. Charles and Caroline Ingalls, for example, were also charter members of this same church.

Margaret continued to support William in their various farming and business endeavors, including helping run their Ferndale mercantile, and helped care for their sight-impaired son, Willie.

Margaret died in Tillamook Country, Oregon, on February 16th, 1908, at the age of seventy-two years old. Her funeral was held at their local Adventist church and she was buried in what is now called Fairview Pioneer Cemetery/Trask Cemetery:

...on February 16, 1908, sadness again descended on both the Owens and Kirry households when Margaret Owens passed away at the age of 72. The last few years had been difficult ones, as her arthritis had become so bad it was hard to do even simple tasks, although Delphia [Willie's wife] was a big help. The funeral was held at the Adventist Church, and she was buried in the Johnson Cemetery (now Fairview Pioneer Cemetery). (Waskin, *Nellie Oleson Story Continues*)

Margaret's obituary appeared in the February 20th, 1908, issue of the *Tillamook Herald*:

Mrs. Margaret H. Owens, wife of Mr. W. H. Owens, died at her home at Long Prairie on Sunday, and the remains were buried on Wednesday, the funeral service being held in the Adventist church, conducted by Rev. W.W. Rosebraugh, the interment being in the Johnson Cemetery. Deceased's maiden name was Margaret H. Gibson, and she was born Jan. 12th, 1836, at Hinchinbook [sic], Huntington county, Province of Quebec, Canada, and on the 20th march, 1864, she was married to Wm. Henry Owens, in Cresco County, Iowa. Some time after they moved to Minnesota, and from there they went to California, and from there they came to Tillamook, the deceased residing here until her death.

At the age of 14 she became a devoted Christian, and since that time had lived a model Christian life. She was a patient kind and loving mother and wife. She leaves a husband and two children, Nellie Kirry, the oldest, who reside at Forest Grove, and Willie, who has lived with his parents on the farm, and Frank, an adopted son, who reside at Cloverdale.

Mrs. Owens was a woman who was greatly loved and respected by all who knew her, and it is with much sorrow that her friends mourn her death and sympathise [sic] with the bereaved husband and family. (Fry-Matson)

Siblings

William Robert Owens (1869-1920)

"Willie" was born a little more than a year after his sister, Nellie, on October 7th, 1869, in Le Roy, Minnesota. He's not just her younger brother, however; Willie has a "Little House" claim to fame in his own right. In the series, the character of Nellie Oleson has a brother called Willie, who was modeled after Willie Owens and is featured in several stories throughout the series.

There was one particular story, however, that didn't make it into the books: Willie went blind in one eye when he was ten, and later, as an adult, he went blind in both.

From the Redwood Falls Gazette, dated July 8th, 1880:

> A terrible accident occurred at this town July 3rd, in which two little boys came near losing their lives. About one o'clock in the afternoon a number of little boys obtained some powder unknown to their parents and were engaged in putting it in an oyster, throwing in a firecracker and then placing a stone over the top of the can and waiting for the explosion. . .The boys had placed the powder in the can, wrapped in paper, and thrown in their lighted firecrackers, which died out, and when they found that was the case, Willie Owens, a little boy of W.H. Owens, aged ten and a half years, lit a match and bent over the can to light the firecracker. The powder of course ignited instantly and he received the contents in his face. (Peterson, 2013)

The result of this accident was that Willie went fully blind in one eye, and had some minor damage to the other. It didn't seem to cripple him, however. He attended school when young, then farmed successfully with his father through 1910. He was still single and living with his parents on the family farm in South Prairie, Tillamook, into his early thirties.

It's important to note that there was no real life "Willie" to model the character of Willie Oleson after beyond Walnut Grove. That was the last place Laura ever saw the Owens' children. Willie was never in De Smet, as both Genevieve Masters and Estella Gilbert (the other two "Nellies") were. Yet the character of Willie appeared in the series there alongside his "sister." It's possible that Laura simply brought Willie Owens' antics from Walnut Grove and placed them in De Smet, or, of course, "Willie" could have been a composite character, too. Perhaps he was modeled after one of the boys in De Smet, or a brother of Estella Gilbert. (Genevieve Masters had no younger siblings.)

On June 16th, 1901, Willie married Philadelphia Ann Watson (April 25th, 1865-October 17th, 1954) in Tillamook. In 1902, their first daughter, Lela was born, followed by two more: Georgia Owens Henry in 1905 and LaVelle Owens Stelzig in 1907. Despite being married and with three children, Willie did not leave the family farm. It's possible that his sight impairment made it impractical, or even impossible, for him to farm alone. Or perhaps it was just a good business relationship for the strong, young son, and the aging father. Whatever the reason, Willie, his family, and his parents were all living together and seemed to be thriving. But shortly after LaVelle's birth, a series of tragedies struck.

While Willie was walking through the family property on his way to a patch of trees to cut some wood, he carried his axe over his shoulder as usual. At some point, the axe got caught on a low hanging branch. When Willie turned to free it, an errant twig pierced his remaining good eye. Though medical care was sought, nothing could be done and his vision was reduced to only ten per cent in that eye, rendering him effectively blind at only thirty-eight years old.

Not long after permanently losing his sight, his beloved mother, Margaret, passed away in 1908. This was a very difficult loss for the family. Their grief, however, was deepened when Willie and Delphia's oldest daughter, Lela, died, just six days after her eighth birthday on May 22nd, 1910.

Within a few years, Willie and Philadelphia had separated, then divorced in 1915, having been married for only fourteen years. It's possible that stress over the full loss of his sight, his mother's death, and the loss of their daughter contributed to the demise of their marriage. All of that grief couldn't have helped but strain their relationship.

An unusual point to note is that Delphia is the third "Kirry" woman, besides her mother-in-law Josephine Kirry and her sister-in-law Nellie Owens Kirry, who listed herself as "widowed" on a census when her ex-husband, Willie, was very much alive. "Divorced" was an option available to women, and they were regularly denoted as such on censuses. So, it's interesting that none of these women chose to answer honestly when the opportunity arrived.

There's another very curious footnote to Willie's story, too. In 1920, Willie was listed on that year's census as living with the family of Fred C. McNelly (or possibly McNally) in Connell, Washington County, Oregon, which is near Forest Grove. He was described on that census as a divorced hired man/farm laborer. By this time, his mother had passed away, he was divorced, and his father was in the Oregon State Insane Asylum. And, most importantly, Willie was *blind*. Yet he was working as a hired man as a farm laborer. How that could have been possible is a mystery.

Sometime in the 1920's, however, Willie decided to enter the newly established Blind Institution in Portland in order to learn new trades. By the time of the 1930 census, he was still living there, age fifty-nine, and "broom maker" was listed as his profession. Willie died of a stroke as he was leaving the school on February 3rd, 1934. He is buried next to his father and sister in the Forest View Cemetery in Forest Grove.

Frank Lester Bedal Owens (1877-1964)

Frank was the adopted son of William and Margaret Owens. He was born on the 23rd of March, 1877, to Lafayette and Clementia Bedal in North Hero Township, Redwood County, Minnesota.

Sadly, Lafayette was killed in a sawmill accident in August of 1882, leaving Clementia and their nine children behind. Poor Frank was only five years old. Because Clementia didn't have the means to care for so many children by herself, many of them were quickly placed with friends and neighbors. Frank came to live with the Owens family in late summer or fall of 1882, to be a companion for partially-sighted Willie. Nellie was fourteen, and Willie was nearly thirteen, so it's strange that a five-year-old boy would have been thought a suitable companion for a young teenager. But, by all accounts, Frank was content living with the Owens family near his mother and siblings.

A year or so later, when the Owens family decided to move to California, Frank was given the option of going with them or staying nearer his birth family. As he was only six, that must have been an excruciating position for him to be in, but his mother, Clementia said he was old enough to make his own decision in the matter.

Little Frank eventually chose to go to California with the Owens, and, though it appears he was never formally adopted, he took their name from around that time. By all accounts, Frank seemed to be happy to be part of the Owens' family. But at some point, he became a little frustrated. "Frank became restless and did not relish his duty as caretaker for young Bill, so at the age of 17, ... he and his friend Jim Whitman, found work building the roads near Woods..." (From an interview with Frank's daughter, Viva)

When Frank was in his early twenties, and the Owens family had moved to South Prairie, Tillamook County, Oregon, Frank got a job hauling cheese from a nearby farm into Tillamook with a four-mule team. While working at this job, he met Eva Elma Nelson (1880-1958) and they were married on April 8th, 1899. Not long afterwards, Frank purchased a plot of his own land and the couple went into dairy farming.

Their first son, Howard Milo Owens, was born on November 4th, 1899, less than seven months after Frank and Eva were married. To put it delicately, Howard was not premature. In the 1900 Federal Census, they're living in Tillamook. In 1903, their son, Arthur Leslie was born, followed by daughters Viva Ruth in (about) 1905, and Edith Elaine in 1907. All of those children were born in Oregon. In 1911, on October 8th, their son, Elmer Bedal, was born in Concord, Contra Costa Country, California, which is in the San Francisco Bay area. They must have returned soon after, however, for when they had Mattie May in 1913, it was in Oregon.

For some reason, between Mattie May's birth in 1913 and the date of the 1920 Federal Census, they decided to try their luck further south again. In the 1920 census, Frank and his family are back in California, this time living in Santa Monica, which is in Southern California, due west of Los Angeles and right on the coast. He's listed as working as a carpenter. But they must have returned once again to Oregon shortly after that census, as twins Ruth Louise and Robert Lloyd were born there in 1921. Unfortunately, Ruth's twin, Robert, died at only sixteen months old. It seems Frank and Eva never lived outside of Oregon again.

In the 1930 and 1940 censuses, Frank is dairy farming in Cloverdale, Oregon, a town he is credited with naming. Frank was very active in the area until his death. Beyond dairy farming, Frank was president of the Tillamook Creamery Association and served as Chairman of the Board in the Cloverdale school system. He also served as the County Commissioner for two terms. He died in 1964, on June 19th. The funeral service was held at the Cloverdale Presbyterian Church and Frank was laid to rest in the IOOF Cemetery in Hebo, Tillamook County, Oregon. (which now appears to be called the Nestucca Valley Community Cemetery.)

Frank was such a respected and integral part of the Cloverdale community, his death made the front page of the Sunday, June 21st, 1964, issue of the Headlight-Herald:

> Pioneer Resident Frank Owens Dies
>
> Frank Lester Owens, 87, passed away Friday morning at Tilla-mook County General hospital following an illness of about six weeks. Services are to be held Monday, June 22, at the Cloverdale Presbyterian church with interment at the 100F cemetery, Hebo.
>
> Mr. Owens had been a Cloverdale resident for 68 years, coming from Walnut Grove, Minn. He was a retired dairy farmer and a member of the Tillamook County Sheriff's Posse, charter member of Cloverdale 100F, served two terms as county commissioner, past president of Tillamook Creamery Association, was chairman of the Cloverdale school board for many years and helped lay the cornerstone of the present courthouse.
>
> Survivors include three daughters, Viva Donaugh and Louise Gilbert, Portland, and Edith Russell, San Francisco, Calif.; three sons, Howard M., Arthur L. and Bill, all of Cloverdale; one brother, Milo Bedal, Seattle; nine grandchildren and 21 great-grandchildren. He was preceded in death by his wife, Eva. (FindAGrave)

GENEVIEVE
MASTERS

GENEVIEVE MAUD MASTERS

Born November 12th, 1867, in Hornby, Steuben County, New York
Died November 7th, 1909, in Chicago, Cook County, Illinois

Genevieve Maude Masters is the second person to make up the "Nellie" character and is the one most responsible for the arrogant and haughty attitude displayed in De Smet in both "Little Town on the Prairie" and "These Happy Golden Years." Unlike Nellie Owens and Estella Gilbert, both of whom came from farming and pioneering families, Genevieve was born in New York State and came from somewhat educated "folk." This background supposedly accounts for her disdain for rough western towns and their simple inhabitants. It appears that she was just the kind of person who enjoyed being rude to others!

The Masters family arrived in De Smet not long after the Ingalls and it's apparent that Laura was very unhappy that they did. She clearly would have preferred that annoying "Gennie" and her family have stayed in Walnut Grove! Back there, Laura had struggled with Genevieve's caustic attitude and sniveling personality. Later in life, she recounted with disgust that "when Genieve got her face washed in the snow she would cry helplessly but I was busy giving as good as I got." (*Pioneer Girl*) Genevieve was prissy. Laura was a tomboy. Oil and water if ever there was!

But it was even more than that. Laura's dislike of Gennie was so profound that she even confessed to having done some things just to spite her. A classmate of theirs in Walnut Grove, Silas Rude, was much admired among the girls for his lovely manners (despite his unfortunate name!). Laura didn't seriously like him, but she sure didn't want Gennie to have his affections!

> Genieve used to watch from her window until she saw him coming, then start to school in time to meet and walk out with him.

Of course, Ma wanted to know why I went down town and I didn't have a good excuse, so she said I should stop being silly over Silas Rude or she would take me out of school. . . .I knew all this but someway I couldn't tell them that I didn't really even like Silas, but I just didn't want Genieve to have his attentions. (*Pioneer Girl*)

Gennie's superior, nasty attitude made for an interesting rivalry between the previous leader of the Walnut Grove girls, Nellie Owens, and Genevieve, as well. With two strong, bossy girls vying for social superiority, the girls in Laura's age group split into two factions. In "Pioneer Girl," Laura recounts:

Genieve sneered at the other girls in school because they were westerners. She thought of herself much above us because she came from New York. She was much nicer dressed than we were and lisped a little when she talked; if she could not have her way in any thing she cried or rather sniveled. Everyone gave up to her and tried to please her because they liked to appear friends with the new girl. Every one that is except Nellie Owens. Nellie was still a leader among the girls when Genieve came and did not intend to give up her leadership. She tried to hold it by being free with candy and bits of ribbon from her father's store. So my crowd divided. . . .I would not be led by either Nellie or Genieve but took sides first with one and then the other as I had a notion, until to my surprise I found myself the leader of them all, because Genieve and Nellie each being eager to win me to her side would play what I wanted to play and do as I said in order to please me.

Though she had ended up "leader" of her chums back in Walnut Grove, in spite of Nellie and Gennie's machinations, Laura was clearly not pleased to see Gennie show up in De Smet:

There were several new girls at school. Mr. Brown had brought his wife and adopted daughter, Ida out in the spring.

Then there was Mary Power daughter of the tailor Tom Power, and Genieve Masters from Walnut Grove. Uncle Sam Masters had come out with his whole family in the spring and taken a homestead west of town.

There was Minnie Johnson and Laura Remington among the younger girls. . .It was hard for me to meet the strange girls and the strange teacher and Genieve was the last unbearable straw.

She was not changed in disposition since the Walnut Grove days. . . (*Pioneer Girl*)

That's a pretty strong statement: "Genevieve was the last unbearable straw." Doesn't leave much room for any interpretation but one, does it? Laura hated Gennie, and hated it even more that she had to deal with her once again.

Did you notice, too, that Minnie Johnson was listed here "among the younger girls?" It was actually Genevieve who was Mary Power's seatmate in school, and, it turns out, her life-long friend. But Laura couldn't have that friendship develop under that character of Nellie Oleson, so she aged Minnie, sat her with Mary Power, and gave haughty "Nellie" a seat of her own. In "Pioneer Girl," Laura states that "Ida Brown and I were still seatmates, as were Mary Power and Genieve Masters." But "Genieve was not popular any more. It was a common saying that, 'her tongue is hung in the middle and runs at both ends' [meaning she was deceitful or false] and not much attention was paid to anything she said."

Laura is clear that this spoiled daughter of Laura's former Walnut Grove teacher, Samuel Masters, is not only responsible for the "De Smet Nellie" character's prickly countenance and conceited voice. . .she is also likely responsible for the physical description that Laura uses. Genevieve was very attractive, with blond hair worn in ringlets of curls, and wore beautifully tailored clothes, though they were made over from eastern relatives' cast-offs. Gennie was also the one who attempted to make friends with the De Smet teacher, Miss Wilder, capitalizing on their connection via their eastern roots, and possibly trying to attract the attention of Almanzo Wilder while doing so.

Both Nellie Owens and Genevieve Masters lived in Walnut Grove, but Nellie Owens did not come west to De Smet. Because of this, it's clear that the stories about Nellie in South Dakota are mostly about Gennie. With very few exceptions, one being the "Nellie in the buggy with Almanzo" tale, in which a story involving Estella Gilbert was told, almost all of the anecdotes about Nellie's insufferable attitude and selfish antics can be attributed directly to Gennie. One of my favorites was particularly memorable. Do you remember when dashing Cap Garland kept trying to give Mary Power some candy, but Nellie kept swooping in and taking it from Cap's hand? This is how Laura explained the real version of that story:

> Genieve. . .was always on hand when Cap brought candy as he often did, a little paper bag full. She asked for it the first time so he gave it to her, with an apologetic look from his blue eyes, under their white lashes, at Mary and me. Genieve passed it once and gobbled the rest.

> After than she would simply take it, pretending she thought it was for her even when he had offered it to Mary, and keeping up a stream of flattering talk. "Cappie was such a dear boy. He was so tall and strong" etc. Cap tried for several days to give the candy to Mary and every time he had to let Genieve have it or be very rude.

> One time I said 'Oh Cap! That's nice of you,' and took it fairly out of Genieve's fingers. Mary and I and Ida ate it all that time and Cap grinned.
>
> Genieve always made fun of Cap behind his back and going home that night she did so saying among other things, 'I like Cap's candy, but Cap! Faugh!' with a curl to her lip and a sniff. (*Pioneer Girl*)

This bold move on Laura's part made the tension between Gennie and Laura even greater. At one point, their relationship took a particularly bad turn and they had their only violent quarrel. Laura remembered:

> Among other things she called attention to my being fat and made fun of my clothes. In return for which I explained to her about the size of her feet, they were very large, and said that at least my clothes were my own and not my aunt's and cousins cast off garments sent to me because I was a poor relation. (*Pioneer Girl*)

In *Little Town on the Prairie*, Laura and the composite Nellie argued, too. Nellie tells Laura:

> I'm glad I don't have to be a teacher. . . . My folks can get along without my having to work." Laura replies, "Of course you needn't, Nellie, but you see, we aren't poor relations being helped out by our folks back East.

The interesting thing about this argument is that it seems to be one of the few incidents where Laura might have mixed the real "Nellies" together to create one singular scene. As far as we know, Nellie Owens wasn't intending to be a teacher when she was young, though she did end up being one many years later in Oregon. So she could easily have made such a snide comment to

Laura. However, she never lived in De Smet, where the comment was supposed to have been made. If it was Nellie Owens who said this, it must have been when Laura and Nellie were living (and fighting!) in Walnut Grove as children. After all, at that time, Nellie Owens' parents were well-off store owners, and it's reasonable to assume that she might have thought that she would never have to "demean" herself with work such as teaching.

Meanwhile, it was Gennie who was in De Smet, and her family was receiving clothes and, perhaps, other help from eastern relatives. So that part of Laura's comment could have been about her. The trouble is, Gennie ended up becoming a teacher and, at the time of this conversation, would probably have already been studying for teacher's exams. Plus, her father was a teacher, so it's highly unlikely that she would have condemned the very profession that her father followed, her mother had worked in, and she, herself, went into!

As Laura's fame as an author grew, endless questions poured in from all over the world about various *Little House* characters, including Nellie. When they did, Laura had an interesting decision to make. In combining three girls into one character, which one would she reference when asked about Nellie? Though there are a few known variations, it was often Genevieve that she referred to, saying that "Nellie Oleson. . .moved back East, and did not live many years." As Gennie did, in fact, end up back east, (well, more east than South Dakota, in the metropolis of Chicago!), and was the "Nellie" who died youngest, at just five days short of her forty-second birthday (Stella Gilbert and Nellie Owens were both eighty when they passed, Stella in Oregon and Nellie in Washington State), Laura was almost certainly talking about the Gennie incarnation of Nellie Oleson.

But she did sometimes make other references, as in a handwritten letter dated May 22nd, 1949, in which she writes to the third and fourth grades at Forston School: "I never saw Nellie after she went east to New York, but I heard she married and went to Oregon and later that she died." It was Gennie who eventually settled in the east in Chicago, though she did live for many years in Washington state first, but it was Nellie Owens who went to Oregon, first living in California for several years, with her family. Only Nellie didn't marry first and then go on to Oregon. . .she married many years after she arrived on the West Coast.

Another letter, this one a typed form letter to children, was dated February of 1947. In it, Laura said "Nellie Oleson married in the East; later separated from her husband and died long ago." None of the "Nellies" married in the east, we're fairly certain. We know for certain that Estella married in De Smet, and Nellie married in Oregon. Though we know that Gennie married in 1888, we've yet to find the exact location, so she's the only possible "eastern" wedding.

But circumstantial evidence would suggest that Gennie had to have been married in De Smet. She was teaching in the area in 1887, her parents were there (on the 1880 census, and during the long winter, and afterwards as Gennie attended the De Smet school in the ensuing years), and then, when Sam Masters died in 1893, five years after Gennie and William married, he was still living in De Smet. Gennie's sister, Augusta, married there in 1888, too, just a few months before Gennie, and both George and Jesse were also living in the area. So Gennie's job and whole family were certainly in De Smet at the time of their nuptials. And, of course, as William had emigrated to the U.S. via Canada, he had no family in the States.

Plus, William had already moved to the west coast and was living on Puget Sound. If he and Gennie would have wed anywhere other than where she grew up and her whole family resided, it would likely have been there, in Washington state, not somewhere east of South Dakota. Therefore, it's highly unlikely that a wedding would have been held anywhere but De Smet.

But only Nellie Owens ended up divorcing her husband. Estella was widowed twice and Gennie died very young, well before her only husband, William. So Laura must have mashed two "Nellies" together in that form letter to schoolchildren, or just plain made a mistake. No single Nellie ended up as she described.

Early Life

Genevieve Maude Masters was born on November 12th, 1867, in Hornby, New York. Her parents, Samuel Oldfield Masters and Margaret Ann Farrington Masters, were farmers at the time with an estate valued at about $9,000.00, which was very respectable for that time period.

But Samuel's background wasn't that of a typical farmer. He has been described as having earned a degree in civil engineering from Cornell University, but Cornell wasn't founded until 1865, and wasn't inaugurated until October 7th, 1868, a year after Genevieve's birth. A later biography about Genevieve's brother, George, only indicates that Samuel was educated in Ithaca, where Cornell was later located, but it does not state "Cornell" specifically. Pamela Smith Hill's side notes about Samuel in "Pioneer Girl" also reference Cornell, though that may have only been an assumption based on George's biography stating "Ithaca" combined with the modern location of Cornell. Prior to Samuel's marrying and having a family, which is the likeliest time for a young man to study for a degree, Cornell was not in existence.

If he wasn't educated at Cornell, however, where else could he have studied? If George's biography is correct, and Samuel did receive a civil engineering degree, AND he did so in Ithaca, we have a problem. The only other college in Ithaca was founded after Cornell.

Samuel is listed as a surveyor in Hornby on the 1860 Federal Census, five years before Cornell was founded. But he's listed as a farmer in 1870 and then again as a surveyor in 1880 in Walnut Grove, so it's possible he worked as a surveyor prior to earning a degree in the subject as an adult. Yet, Hornby is forty miles from Cornell, which is too far to commute, and it would have been highly unlikely for a married man with a large family to leave them to go study for a degree.

We do know that Samuel worked at various times as a school administrator, merchant, and surveyor in New York, so it is likely that he had higher education of some kind. Margaret, herself, was educated, too, and had been employed as a schoolteacher before she married Samuel.

Gennie was the youngest of the four Masters' children by far. Her oldest brother, George was fifteen years her elder, Augusta, who later went by her middle name of "Elgetha," was nine years older, and her brother, Jesse, was four years older.

In the 1870 census, the Masters were still living in Hornby, however, later that year, Samuel moved the family to nearby Corning. On that 1870 census, Samuel was still farming and George, who was then about seventeen, was listed as a farm laborer. Gussie was eleven and attending school. Jesse was six and Gennie was only two. It was in the town of Corning, New York, where Gennie first started the "eastern education" she was so fond of referencing later in Walnut Grove and De Smet.

She didn't enjoy too many years of her fancy eastern education, however, as the family made another move, this time to Walnut Grove, Minnesota, in 1878, when Gennie was about eleven years old. This is where the first connection to the Ingalls occurs. Samuel taught the school where both Gennie and the Ingalls girls attended, and Laura did not like either Samuel or his daughter much at all.

Walnut Grove is also where the Masters family seems to first split up, and there's a bit of a mystery as to what, exactly, happened. By 1880, Gennie was the only one of her siblings still living with her parents. For George, that's not surprising as he was so much older than Gennie. In 1880, he was twenty-seven years old and married. He was also living in De Smet (so he went there before his parents did).

Augusta was a mystery for a while as she was hard to find on any historical record for the time period. She wasn't married until 1888, but she wasn't with her family in Walnut Grove, either. Yet she appeared in later documents, so she hadn't died. We searched for Augusta, and Elgetha, but that yielded nothing. When we finally searched under "Gussie," however, the mystery was solved. Under that nickname, she was listed as boarding and teaching in North Hero Township, Minnesota, not far from Walnut Grove. (Historical research would be much easier if given names, properly spelled, would have been consistent on official records!)

Brother Jesse, however, was another Masters child not living with his family on the 1880 census, and he would only have been about sixteen years old. Like Augusta, he ends up back in De Smet as an adult, but where he was during the 1880 census remains a mystery. We spotted a possible "Jesse Masters" in West Virginia, though that's a very long way away from Dakota territory! He's listed as a border and a scholar, but the age and birth information is a little off. Mistakes were often made on official census documents, but, even so, it's not a particularly strong match. The only real possible linking evidence is the name, the circumstantial fact that he wasn't with his family in Walnut Grove at a relatively young age, the fact that his father was supposed to have had a university education and might have wanted him to have a similar opportunity, and the rough age. But it's certainly far from conclusive. Sixteen-year-old boys typically still lived with their parents.

Wherever Jesse had disappeared to, however, Gennie was living with her folks in Walnut Grove and attending school there. In Walnut Grove, Samuel worked as both a surveyor and, as we've already mentioned, a school teacher. Laura frequently referred to him as "Uncle Sam" because of his name and likeness to the same. She did not like Mr. Masters as a teacher.

Just a few years later, Samuel made his last move, bringing the family to De Smet, South Dakota in either 1880 or 1881. Most sources cite the latter date, believing Samuel, Margaret, and Gennie arrived after the "Long Winter" of 1880-1881. According to the 1880 census, which was taken on June 16th, the family was still in Walnut Grove, so 1881 is the likelier year they arrived in De Smet. George, however, was definitely in De Smet during the "Long Winter." Though it didn't appear in the books, George and his wife lived with the Ingalls family during that hard winter.

Gennie finished her education in De Smet, then taught many school terms in the local area, first in Hamlin County and then she took over the Wilkin School (not the "Wilkins" school!) after Laura had taught there in the spring of 1885.

The Wilkin School, which was formally known as "Common School No. 6," was brand new when Laura taught there, having been built in the first part of April just after Laura had taken her teacher's exams. It was located slightly east of Thomas Wilkin's homestead. (Thomas was the father of Laura's friend and classmate, Florence Wilkin, and an architect by trade.) The school land didn't border the Wilkin property directly, but it did border Almanzo Wilder's tree claim. One corner of the school plot also met with the corner of Eliza Jane Wilder's tree claim, and Royal Wilder's tree claim was just a few plots away, as well.

Laura's spring term was a three-month school from late April to July and she wasn't paid, as she reported in "These Happy Golden Years," thirty dollars per month (less two dollars per week boarding with her friend, Florence, who would have been offered the position if she'd passed her exams!). The salary was actually just twenty-five dollars, and, considering that Gennie taught the next term after Laura, probably would have been what she earned, too.

It's interesting to me that the money wasn't as good as Laura could have earned elsewhere, especially when you subtract about eight dollars per month for room and board. . .that's one third of her total income! Interesting, too, that the location of the school was right next to Almanzo's tree claim, where he built their first home together. Even more interesting still because Laura had an admitted history of attempting to thwart the romantic notions of Genevieve (remember Silas Rude?)! Was Laura's taking a job with less net pay right before she married a tactical move to keep Genevieve away from Almanzo? Hmmm!

If that was her plan, it worked well and Laura and Almanzo married in August of 1885. Genevieve taught the next three terms of the Wilkin School directly adjacent to the Wilder's new home on Almanzo's tree claim. Given the animosity between Laura and Gennie, I wonder how that must have felt for the two women to have been in such close proximity.

Preemption of Henry Hopp	Homestead of Sterr	Homestead of Bauer	Homestead of Starr	Tree Claim of Armstrong	Homestead of Reilly
Homestead of Killoren	Tree Claim of Trone	Homestead of Trone	**Tree Claim of Royal Wilder**	Homestead of Taylor	Homestead of Hainstock
Preemption of Killoren	Preemption of Larabee & Tree Claim of Wells	Homestead of Fuller	Homestead of Webb	Homestead of O. Sands	Homestead of G. Sands
Homestead of McMartin		Homestead of E. Raymond	**Tree Claim of Eliza Jane Wilder**	Homestead of VanHook	**Tree Claim of Almanzo J. Wilder**
Preemption of T. Wells	Homestead of J. Wells	**Homestead of T.C. Wilkin**	Homestead of G.C.R. Fuller	**SCHOOL LAND**	
Homestead of H. Chase	Homestead of Loftus	Homestead of Rock	Homestead of James Glover		

(Cleaveland, 2015)

After three terms teaching at the Wilkin School, Genevieve left De Smet to attend Pierre University (Pierre, Dakota Territory) in the fall of 1886, and taught both grammar and United States history locally as part of her one year course. The fledgling University had a bit of a tumultuous start. Pierre University was founded in 1883 as the Presbyterian University of Southern Dakota. A year later, it was renamed Pierre University, though it was commonly called Pierre College. The University awarded the first degree in Dakota Territory on May 31st, 1887. It is likely, therefore, that Gennie was part of the first formal graduating class. Due to financial problems, the University moved to Huron about eleven years later, in 1898.

After her return to Kingsbury County in 1887, Gennie taught in a school near Spring Lake for a term, then in another new school just southwest of De Smet. During this time, she also was responsible for the instruction of "reading in the classroom" at various teachers' institutes in Kingsbury County. So, it's clear that Genevieve was a very experienced, educated, and accomplished teacher.

Married Life and Death

Of all the "Nellies," Genevieve's life after De Smet is possibly the most dramatic and intriguing. She married William Graham V. Renwick on September 11th, 1888, probably in De Smet, though that's not confirmed. Circumstantial evidence is strong, however: Gennie had been working in Kingsbury County as a teacher, her family resided in De Smet, William had no family in the U.S., and De Smet is where he had met Gennie when he first came in 1886 as an agent of Youmans Bros. & Hodgins Lumber Company of Winona, Minnesota. So it certainly seems the most likely wedding location.

William emigrated, first to Canada in 1881, then to America in 1884, from the UK. The shocking story (for the time) of Nellie Owens' divorce was nothing compared to the story of William and Gennie, however! Their marriage was fraught with lies, embezzlement, and, of course, tragedy.

The most circulated story of William is that he was born in Scotland in December of 1861, came to the U.S. in 1884, and was a prominent and respected citizen. A short biography in "An Illustrated History of the State of Washington" (1893) elaborates:

> W.G.V. RENWICK, professional accountant, Spokane, Washington, was born in Aberdeen, Scotland, December 25, 1861. His father, a clergyman, was a native of Northumberland, England, and his mother was a descendant of the ill-fated house of Stuarts.

> The subject of our sketch received his preparatory education at Rugby. He then took a classical course at Clifton University and also studied theology. Leaving school before he completed his course, be went to sea as purser in the merchant marine service. In 1881 he came to America and located at Winnipeg during the boom in Manitoba, and while there was engaged in speculating and farming. He came to the United States in 1884

and settled in Wisconsin, turning his attention to the lumber business for a time. In 1887 he again directed his course westward, and took up his abode at Puget Sound. He entered the service of Pierce county, as accountant, and established a system of county bookkeeping that was considered the most efficient of all in the State. He revised the books of Pierce county in such a manner that his work was most favorably commented upon and attracted wide-spread attention. About this time the county of Spokane required the service of and expert accountant, and at the earnest request of Judge J.J. Peel, Mr. Renwick came to Spokane in May, 1891, and took charge of the books, and as the result of his efficient work Spokane is considered the banner county of the State as regards its books.

Mr. Renwick was married in 1888, to Genevieve Maude Masters, a native of Corning, New York. He is a member and one of the choristers of the Episcopal Church.

That all looks fairly impressive, doesn't it? Mom descended from the House of Stuarts, Dad a respectable clergyman? A classical and theological education at Rugby and Clifton? Member of the local Episcopal church and choir? Wow. So, of course, it stands to reason that this quality, educated individual would be capable of setting the accounting standards of a prominent American county!

The trouble is, his background doesn't really add up. A clergyman, while respectable, didn't earn a huge amount of money in the mid-1800's UK, and Rugby was an exclusive preparatory school (which was education prior to university, so the equivalent of junior and senior high school in the U.S.) and was extremely expensive. Prime Ministers' sons attended Rugby. Sons of Lords and other ridiculously wealthy land-owners attended Rugby. The sons of regular clergymen from Scotland with modest incomes typically did not.

Nor is the likeliest "Clifton University" (Bristol University, but located in Clifton) the expected caliber a Rugby student would then attend, especially as the University's focus was on medicine and engineering rather than "classical education." Rugby students tended to go on to prestigious schools like Oxford or Cambridge. And isn't it odd that with such an impressive preparatory and university education, that he ended up in the merchant marines? It would seem more logical for a well-off, well-educated man to simply buy his passage to North America. It all sounds a little suspect.

There's something else, too. He seems to have quite a few birth dates floating around that appear to conflict. The "Illustrated History of the State of Washington" bio noted December 25th, 1861, as his date of birth, but his gravestone has the year 1862 inscribed on it, though it has no month or day. Findagrave.com gives the month, day, and year of his birth as October 16th, 1862. In the 1900 census, however, William, himself, gives his birth month and year as December, 1862, both of which are confirmed in a bio of Gennie in the book "Education in Kingsbury County," though Edinburgh is noted as his place of birth, not Aberdeen. On another official document, however, William's Illinois death record, we have yet another date: October 16th, 1864. That's three possible birth years, and two possible birth days, two possible birth months, and a couple of possible birthplaces, too.

So, what is correct, and why all the confusion?

To be honest, it's difficult to tell. A rather intense search for a William G. V. Renwick using the story he told of himself. . .being born in Aberdeen, son of a clergyman, attending Rugby and then Clifton. . .yields no results. No Scottish or English census information. No birth records. No historical mention of any kind. Given the supposed prominence of his background, that's also a little suspicious.

There is one possible hit for a William Renwick in Scotland, however. In the *Illinois Deaths and Stillbirths Index*, his father is listed as Walter Renwick, born in Newcastle, England, and his mother was Anna Grey, born in Scotland. There is a Walter and Anna (Anne) Gray Renwick found in Scotland in the right time period, and they did, indeed, have a son called William. However, this Walter was a merchant, not a clergyman. And this William Renwick was born on April 8th, 1860, in Leith, Midlothian, Scotland, which is greater Edinburgh, not Aberdeen. Edinburgh was one of our possible birthplaces.

Considering there is only one Walter and Anna (Gray) Renwick with a son called William in Scotland (or England, for that matter) in that time period, it seems likely that this is the correct family. But it's certainly not the impressive background that William described. And his actual birthdate is not what any of the American sources claim.

His story shifts in another place, too. On the 1889 Washington Territorial Census for Pierce County, for example, William claimed he was born in England. Given that William, himself, provided this information, it's strange that he wouldn't correctly report the country of his own birth which previously had been Scotland.

Of course, after arriving in America, there's no doubt William must have been good at each position he held, first in the lumber industry, and later in accounting, as he steadily climbed the ladder of success. Impressing people all along the way, he was even head-hunted out of his first accounting position in Pierce County (on Puget Sound) by the eastern Washington county of Spokane. Between these two jobs, the first starting in 1887, and the Spokane position starting in May, 1891, William found time to return eastward and marry Genevieve in September of 1888. According to that complimentary bio in "An Illustrated History of the State of Washington," William was a stellar employee who enjoyed tremendous success and prominence in his field. Newly wed and with his career soaring, you'd think Gennie and William had it all.

However, that's not the way it played out. William's unprovable and varying past might have been a cover for a rather slippery and unethical man. Just a year or two after that glowing "Illustrated History" entry, William Renwick was indicted in Spokane on several counts of embezzlement. In March of 1885, Judge Buck sentenced William on the first count to two years of hard labor in what is now called the Washington State Penitentiary, in Walla Walla. Because William pleaded guilty, appeared repentant, and it was his first offence, the sentence was relatively light and the remaining multiple charges were dropped. He served three-fourths of his prison sentence, allowing for "good conduct credits," before being pardoned. In the "House Journal of the Fifth Legislature of the State of Washington," the case is described:

> WGV Renwick, having pled guilty to the crime of embezzlement, was on the 4th day of March, 1895, sentenced by the superior court of Spokane county to imprisonment for the term of two years. Pardon granted March 16, 1896, upon the recommendation of the trial judge, general attorney of the state, the prosecuting attorney in the case, the board of county commissioners, and many officials and citizens of Spokane city and county.
>
> Renwick has a wife in delicate health and dependent upon him for support. At the time pardon was granted it was represented that he could secure remunerative employment.

Where Gennie resided while William was incarcerated, we don't know. Because of the nature of her situation, and the distance from her family, she might have "hid" somewhere on the west coast while he was in prison, living on savings or, perhaps, even his ill-gotten gains. None of the news articles about the case or the

House Journals make mention of whether William was required to repay what he embezzled, though one would hope that he was. On the one count he was actually sentenced for, he'd embezzled two hundred and six dollars. That's worth several thousand dollars in today's money. (Remember that Laura paid two dollars per week for her room and board at the Wilkin's home.) We don't know whether each count was for more or less, or how many counts against him there originally were—references only say things like "many" and "several." But we're likely talking in the many-hundreds-of-dollars stolen, if not thousands, which could easily have supported Genevieve lavishly while William was in prison.

Of course, if they did have to return that money, she would have been left with no way to support herself while he was incarcerated. And without a source of income, and the support of her husband, she might have been forced to return to De Smet to live with family. That would have been a very embarrassing and emotionally difficult option. Explaining why her husband was imprisoned might have been more than she could do.

Wherever Gennie was during that long year, it's no surprise that as soon as William was released from prison, he and Gennie left their shame and troubles in Washington and headed east to begin again. What is surprising, however, is that William had the chutzpah, and, frankly, the opportunity, to re-enter the field of accounting. And, by all accounts, was again extremely successful.

By 1900, William and Gennie were living on South Turner Avenue in Chicago in a rented house. William was working as an accountant at 204 Dearborn, which was in the commercial and banking hub of Chicago. Their new baby girl, and only child, Margaret, had been born in April of that year, twelve years after William and Gennie were first married.

The Renwicks didn't live happily ever after, however. In the summer of 1909, when Gennie was only forty-one, she decided to visit her old friend, and school seatmate, Mary Power Sanford, who then lived in Bellingham, Washington. On the way home from that visit, she stayed in De Smet for several weeks before finishing her journey back to Chicago. Toward the end of her trip, Gennie caught a cold which then, sadly, turned into pneumonia. She died on November 7th, 1909, leaving William and her nine-year-old daughter behind, and was buried in De Smet Cemetery. Her obituary, which was published in the De Smet News on November 12th, 1909, fills in the details:

> Again We Mourn. Great was the shock that came to the editor's family and relatives last Monday in the news that Mrs. W.G. Renwick had succumbed to pneumonia at her home in Chicago after but a few days illness. Mrs. Renwick and daughter Margaret stopped here on their way home from the Pacific Coast where they had spent the summer with friends in Seattle, Bellingham, and Spokane. After a couple of weeks visit they left for home on the 30th accompanied by the mother, Mrs. Margaret Masters. Mrs. Renwick had contracted a severe cold and was quite ill on the way and on arrival in Chicago was put in the hands of the family physician. Nothing serious was feared for several days, but the case became serious and a specialist was called in but physicians and nurses could do nothing and death came Sunday evening, November 7th at eight o'clock.
>
> The remains were brought to DeSmet for burial, arriving here Tuesday evening accompanied by the husband, mother and daughter, and Mrs. Mary M. Blodgett and Mr. A.B. Leith, long time friends of the family. Funeral services were held Wednesday morning in St. Stephens Episcopal church, the beautiful burial service being read by the rector, Mr. Randall. The choir was composed of Mr. and Mrs. Hamilton, Miss Eggleston and Dr. Hall with J.H. Carroll as conductor.

Genevieve Masters was born in Hornby, New York, Nov. 12, 1867. She was the daughter of Mr. and Mrs. Samuel O. Masters, the youngest of four children. Two years later the family moved to Corning, N.Y. where they lived eight years. In 1878 they came west, locating in Walnut Grove, Minn. and in 1881 settled on a farm near DeSmet. On September 11, 1888 Miss Masters was married to Mr. W.G. Renwick. One daughter was born to them, Margaret now aged nine. For thirteen years the home has been in Chicago. Geo. E. Masters of Spencer and Mrs. C.P. Sherwood and J.F.B. Masters of DeSmet with the aged mother are the surviving members of the Masters family who with the husband and daughter and other relatives are called upon to mourn the departure of their loved one. The mysterious ways of Providence are past finding out.

Little Margaret Renwick is for the present at least to make her home with her aunt, Mrs. Sherwood. Mr. and Mrs. Geo. E Masters and daughters Juanita and Hazel of Spencer and son Claude of Humboldt came Tuesday to attend the funeral of Mrs. Renwick, returning Thursday.

By 1910, the year following Genevieve's death, William was living on 615 South Ashland Blvd, Chicago, but now working as an accountant, this time at 180 LaSalle, which was only a couple of blocks away from the location of his Dearborn job in 1900. South Ashland Boulevard has been described as one of the finest residential streets in the West Division of Chicago during that era, complete with several elegant mansions. However, despite clearly having room enough, William did not have Margaret living with him. Instead, she was living back in De Smet with Gennie's sister, Augusta. We can find no evidence that they ever lived together again.

In the 1911 Chicago City Directory, William was still on South Ashland Boulevard and was still listed as an accountant. In the 1913 Chicago City Directory, however, he was then a credit manager, working at 216 Monadnock Block, which was a skyscraper in the main commercial hub of Chicago. The only bankers that were listed at this address during this time period were A.W. Jefferis and Co., which we presume were his employers.

By 1920, however, William had moved to Aurora, Illinois, which is not too far outside of Chicago. He was an accountant again, this time for Kirby Cullen & Co., a firm of Certified Public Accountants. He does not appear in the 1923 City Directory for Aurora, however, so his time there must have been fairly short.

He died back in Chicago, Cook County, Illinois on March 5th, 1924, at the age of fifty-nine, or, if the William we found in Scotland was really him, sixty-four. He never remarried after Gennie's premature death. And, despite nearly thirty years of living and working in and near Chicago, William chose to be laid to rest near his wife. He was buried in De Smet, South Dakota on March 8th, 1924, just three short days after his death.

Family

Children

Gennie and William had only one daughter, **Margaret E. Renwick**. Margaret was born in Chicago, Cook County, Illinois, on April 24th, 1900. According to the Michigan Death Index, she died December 23rd, 1982, in Mansfield, Iron County, Michigan. The Social Security Death Index, however, lists her last place of residence as Channing, Dickinson, Michigan. They're not far apart, however, so it's possible that both are correct.

Margaret's middle name remains a mystery, but as her aunt, Augusta Masters Sherwood, had the middle name of Elgetha, that's a likely option. Augusta was Gennie's only sister, and she's the one who took nine-year-old Margaret in after Gennie died, so it wouldn't be surprising to have a same-middle-name connection.

Both the 1910 and 1920 censuses show Margaret living with her Aunt Augusta, Uncle Carter P. Sherwood, and her cousins. One of those cousins was Aubrey Howells Sherwood, who eventually became the editor of the De Smet news and the co-founder of the Laura Ingalls Wilder Memorial Society. Given his Aunt Gennie was one of the "Nellies," that's a particularly appropriate connection.

We cannot find any evidence that William interacted much with his daughter after Gennie's death, but of course, that's hard to establish, either way. It's possible that Gennie had confided in her family about William's legal troubles, and they didn't think he was morally fit to raise Margaret. Of course, it's also possible that William just felt that his young daughter simply needed a family and a mother figure, and so letting Augusta raise her was simply in Margaret's best interest.

Later in life, Laura mentioned the embezzlement scandal in a letter to her daughter, Rose. If she had heard about it, given she was certainly not a confidante of Genevieve, it must have come through De Smet gossip. And if the townsfolk of De Smet had heard about it, it's likely that William wouldn't have been a particularly welcome figure in the town. If so, Margaret must have effectively lost her father, not just her mother, when she was only nine.

Eventually, Margaret grew up and married Leonard ("Lars") A. Thune on August 8th, 1925, in Blue Earth County, Minnesota, about seventeen months after the death of her father. Lars and Margaret's daughter, Joan Thune, was born November 4th, 1929 (died July 15th, 1996) and married Martin Waananen. Their son, John Renwick Thune, was born November 19th, 1932 (died May 29th, 2006). He married Elizabeth Swaine.

Margaret was employed as a teacher at Howe Elementary school, the oldest surviving school in Green Bay.

Grandparents

Genevieve's paternal grandparents were **Nehemiah and Harriet Masters**. Nehemiah was born on March 8th, 1792, in Sussex County, New Jersey, and died on December 23rd, 1863, in Hornby, Steuben, New York. Harriet Mather Masters was born on February 10th, 1797, in Orange County, New York, and died on February 23rd, 1862, in Hornby, as well. They were married on February 15th, 1818, in Steuben County, New York.

Genevieve's maternal grandparents were **Isaac and Phebe Farrington**. Isaac was born in 1801 in Yonkers, Westchester, New York and died in 1850 (possibly June) in Hornby, Steuben, New York. Phebe (Phoebe) Bartine Farrington was born on January 10th, 1800, in Westchester, New York. She died in Steuben County as well, in 1895.

Parents

Genevieve's father was **Samuel Oldfield Masters**, and he seemed to be quite a character. Born on June 19th, 1822, in Wantage, Sussex County, New Jersey, he married Margaret Ann Farrington on March 25th, 1852, in New York State and they had four children together, the youngest of which was Gennie. Samuel was, at various times, a town clerk, a surveyor, a farmer, a schoolteacher, a principal, a merchant, and even an inventor. According to an annotation in *Pioneer Girl*, Samuel Masters received a degree in civil engineering from Cornell University, though that has been drawn into doubt. But he did very well in a number of professions, so it is likely he did have some kind of formal educational background. His brother, William Masters, owned the Masters hotel in Burr Oak that the Ingalls helped run for a while and later opened another hotel in De Smet. Apparently, Samuel's appearance was so similar to the popular symbol of America that Laura called him "Uncle Sam." She didn't like him very much when he taught her in Walnut Grove:

> Our teacher this spring and summer was Mr. Master's brother. We all called him "Uncle Sam." He was tall and thin, with bad teeth and a bad breath and small brown eyes and a bald head. He had an unpleasant habit of putting his face to[sic] close to ours when he talked to us and would absent-mindedly pick up and fondle any of the girls hands that happened to be happy. He captured mine one day when I had a pin in my fingers and I turned the pin quickly, so it jabbed deep when he squeezed. After than he let my hands alone. (*Pioneer Girl*)

Bad breath and bad manners aside, he was a pretty intelligent and accomplished man. He even managed to invent an interesting contraption:

Uncle Sam Masters had invented a machine he said would find gold, silver, or iron wherever it was. . .It did so well that Mr. Masters [Samuel's brother] had him try it out in the pasture. . .And sure enough Uncle Sam's instrument said there was on the far bank of a dry wash a little ways back of our house. . .When the drill had gone down a hundred feet, it was blown out of the hole and a stream of water followed it. . .The water ran out the top of the pipe into a barrel, overflowed from that and ran off making a little brook out of what had been the dry wash. The water tasted strong of iron and turned everything it ran over a rusty red, so Pa and Mr Masters thought likely there was iron ore down in the ground. (*Pioneer Girl*)

He never found a gold mine, however, and Samuel died on August 15th, 1893, in De Smet, Kingsbury County, South Dakota. He's buried in the De Smet Cemetery.

Genevieve's mother was **Margaret Ann Farrington**. Though her gravestone says she was born in 1828, she was actually born on September 10th, 1827, in Liberty, Sullivan County, New York. After marrying Samuel in 1852, Margaret gave birth to their son, George, in 1853, their daughter, Augusta, in 1859, their son, Jesse, in 1864, and, finally, to Genevieve in 1867. This is an unusually large spread in years from the first child to the last. . .four children spread over fourteen years! The 1910 census notes that she only gave birth to these four children, with one having died (Gennie), which makes the time between children unusual. Typically, such long gaps would have indicated several miscarriages or infant/toddler deaths. This, thankfully, didn't seem to be the case with Margaret. . .she just spaced them out!

She died in De Smet, on March 22nd, 1915, where she is also buried in the De Smet Cemetery. She outlived her youngest child, Genevieve, by more than five years.

Siblings

George Emmett Masters (1853 – 1913)

George was born in Steuben county, New York, on February 26th, 1853. He married Margaret White Gilmore (or Gilmour) (February 28th, 1953-June 25th, 1913) in 1879, but the exact date is uncertain. According to a short biography we found, they married in July of 1879, and their son, Arthur Kingsbury Masters, was born on May 23rd, 1880. Arthur was said to be the first white child born in De Smet.

But those dates don't add up. If George and Margaret had really been married in July of 1879, Laura would likely not have written the following in a letter to her daughter, Rose, about their living with them during the long winter:

> When Maggie came Ma saw she would soon have a baby, much too soon after the time she was married.
>
> Maggie didn't want the baby to be born at her folk's and disgrace them. George's folks were mad because he married her and wouldn't have her at their house.
>
> Maggie had always been a nice girl and Ma was sorry for her and let her stay. The baby was born before winter came. . .Work stopped and George came. . .The winter set in and caught them. There was nowhere else they could stay. . . (*Selected Letters*, p.166-167)

Augusta Elgetha Masters Sherwood (1859-1927)

Genevieve's only sister, Augusta, was born on the 4th of April, 1859, in Steuben County, New York. She married Carter Parsons Sherwood (August 8th, 1862-October 18th, 1929) on April 11th, 1888, just a few months before Gennie married William.

Augusta, who by then went by her middle name of Elgetha, and Carter had three children together: Vincent Masters Sherwood (March 25th, 1889-June 1972), Reginald Carter Sherwood (August 6th, 1891-May 18th, 1981), and Aubrey Howells Sherwood (November 7th, 1894-December 19th, 1987). Elgetha took her niece, Margaret Masters, in after the death of Gennie and raised her into adulthood.

Elgetha died in De Smet on January 12th, 1927, and is buried there, too.

Jesse Farrington B. (Bartine?) Masters (1864-1963)

Genevieve's older brother, Jesse, was born in May of 1864 in Steuben County, New York. He has, however, a slightly confusing trail through the censuses. He's living with the family in Hornby, New York, in 1870, when he's just six. But there is no trace of him living with his family in the 1880 census, when he would have been sixteen. Some early researchers surmised that meant he had died. The 1890 Federal Census was lost, so that is not an available resource. The next possible census was in 1900, and there Jesse did turn up again, alive and well at thirty-six, living in De Smet and farming. He's with his wife, Anna M. Masters, whom he married in 1895, and has a homestead patent for land just northeast of De Smet, dated 1889.

Why Jesse was not living with his family on the 1880 census, when he would have only been about sixteen years old, remains a mystery. Although, as we said earlier, we found a listing for a "Jesse Masters" in West Virginia, living as a boarder and listed as a scholar, during that time period, it's not a particularly strong match.

There's a strange thing about his wife, too. Anna's age changes a great deal throughout the various censuses. When she first appears with Jesse, he is thirty-six and she is thirty-five. By 1910, their ages were the same, and they're listed as forty-six. By the 1920 census, however, Anna has leapt ahead, being listed as sixty, while Jesse is fifty-five. By the time the 1940 census rolls around, she is listed a full eight years older. Another document lists her as ten years older!

One further mystery is that, on the 1930 census, the "age at first marriage" for Jesse is thirty-two, which seems to be correct. But Anna's "age at first marriage" is eighteen! If her later census birthdates are correct, there is no way that Jesse could have been her first marriage (he would have been only eight years old when she was eighteen!). But we can find no record of her being married before Jesse. It's possible, however, as she and Jesse had only one child, who did not survive, that her first marriage ended because she couldn't have children. It's intriguing, at any rate!

Jesse died on June 10th, 1963, in De Smet, where he is also buried.

ESTELLA GILBERT

ESTELLA M. GILBERT

Born May, 1864, in Lake City, Wabasha County, Minnesota
Died September 16th, 1944, in Yakima, Yakima County, Washington

The third and final person included in the character of Nellie was Estella M. Gilbert. There are a few minor mysteries surrounding her connection to the *Little House* stories, though I confess this makes her one of the more intriguing figures in the Nellie triad to me. Laura, herself, seemed a bit muddled about the details of the Gilbert family when she described their connection in her later years. One thing, however, she was not cloudy about: the real-life Stella was responsible for one of the juiciest De Smet storyline, the love-triangle buggy story involving Almanzo, which appeared in "These Happy Golden Years."

Trying to keep the story uncluttered with too many moving parts, Laura decided, as she did with Genevieve, to drape Stella's (mis)deeds in Nellie's persona. The act was a deliberate narrative choice. In a letter to Rose, dated August 17th, 1938, Laura discussed the characters who would appear in De Smet. She confided that the new friends would "be Mary Power and Ida Brown, perhaps Stella Gilbert. Though I think I'll combine Jennie [Genevieve Masters] and Stella in Nellie Oleson." (*Selected Letters*)

Stella didn't seem to be as mean as the character of Nellie had become. In fact, there doesn't seem to be much evidence that she was a haughty, rude person at all. According to Laura, her two main character flaws seemed to be that she was a bit lazy and she eventually developed an eye for Almanzo. Hardly mortal flaws. So, it's likely that the personality of Nellie's character was Genevieve's, and only an event or two, were based on Stella.

Laura and Stella's beginnings were not out on the prairie in De Smet, however. They began about three hundred miles east on the banks of the Mississippi river. Stella was born only a few miles across Lake Pepin (which is just a wide portion of the Mississippi) from Laura's home in Pepin, Wisconsin. Laura never mentions this early connection, however, and, given the lake was only crossable when frozen enough to bear the weight of a wagon or via a ferry when the ice was melted, that could easily be accounted for by the close-but-yet-so-far nature of their geographical locations.

Except. . .

They not only knew each other, they actually attended the same school between 1871 and 1873. The Laura Ingalls Wilder Memorial Society in De Smet holds records showing that both the Gilberts and the Ingalls attended the Barry Corner School, which was only about a mile from the Ingalls' home.

Hazel Gilbert Failing (Stella's niece by her older brother, David) confirmed the connection. In *Lore*, volume 6 number 2, Hazel is credited with tracing "back the long friendship of the Ingalls and the Gilberts – way back to Wisconsin, when her grandparents lived in the Pepin area and across the lake at Lake City, Minnesota. A faded old photo of a log cabin school in the woods shows the Gilberts and Ingalls as classmates, long before the families were reunited on the prairies."

Laura was pretty young during that time, however, which might account for her mistakes and lack of memory about knowing the Gilberts in Pepin. John E. Miller, in his biography, *Becoming Laura Ingalls Wilder: The Woman Behind the Legend*, explains that connection more fully:

> Since she had turned six by the time the family returned to Wisconsin, [Laura's older sister] Mary was enrolled for the summer term in the Barry Corner School. The schoolhouse was only about half a mile down the road from their cabin. The teacher, Anna Barry, lived nearby with her parents, after whom the crossroads was named. They had been among the earliest arrivals in the area, coming from near Pittsburgh, Pennsylvania, during the mid-1850s. Among the twenty students enrolled for

the term besides Mary were Uncle Henry and Aunt Polly's four children as well as Clarence Huleatt.

Laura was lonesome, and perhaps slightly jealous, when Mary went to school, leaving her home in the cabin with her mother and little sister while her father was often hunting or working in the fields. In October, when the fall term started, her parents allowed her to go to school with Mary, even though she was still only four years old. The experiment lasted only until Christmas, however, and after that Laura was kept home from school until she was a little older.

Because of her age, it's possible that Laura was too young to remember the Gilberts. But Mary, Ma, and Pa were not, and it would seem likely to be a solid point of connection and topic of conversation when the two families eventually reconnected three hundred miles west on the prairie. So why did Laura state that she only got acquainted with Stella in De Smet? And when she spoke of the Gilbert family arriving in De Smet, why was her account fraught with so many errors? In *Pioneer Girl*, Laura wrote:

> Some people named Gilbert lived on a farm north and east of town. There were Pa and Ma Gilbert, Al and Fred and Stella and Leona Gilbert.
>
> They had come early in the spring after the hard winter and by the next winter Ma Gilbert had become bedridden and had not been out of her bed since though she looked well enough, with bright eyes and color in her cheeks.
>
> Stella and her father did the work and cared for Leona who had been born since her mother refused to try to get up.
>
> I got acquainted with Stella at Sunday-school and had been out to the house and seen the rest of the family. Now Fred was going to school and seemed to want to be very attentive to me.

In an annotation to Laura's statement, however, Pamela Smith Hill wrote:

> Contrary to what Wilder remembered, the family had arrived in Kingsbury County prior to the hard winter. In fact, nineteen-year-old David A. Gilbert, the second son in the family, was the mail carrier who outraces a blizzard and safely delivers the mail from Preston in The Long Winter. Stella was about 3 years older than Wilder; Fred was about Wilder's age.

Beyond Hill's correct catch about the timing of the Gilberts' arrival in Kingsbury County, there are a few further errors and omissions in Laura's statement. The Gilberts' last baby was not named "Leona," but, rather, "Luella." And Laura missed out three of the Gilbert siblings, whom she should have known if she'd "been out to the house and seen the rest of the family." Stella's oldest brother, Christopher, was already making his own way in the world, and wasn't living with the family, so Laura got the next three correct as she named David (who was also called "Al" as a shortened version of his middle name, Allison), Stella, and Fred (who also went by his middle name). But between Fred and Luella (Leona) were three more Gilberts: Charles Nathan, Elizabeth Ann, and Ada Mae. That's a lot of kids to miss, especially since Charles Nathan was only a few years younger than Laura, and would likely have been at school with her.

The final error was that Laura and Stella got acquainted at Sunday School. While it's possible that she never really connected with Stella on any personal level back in the Pepin area, since they were three years apart in age, it still seems a strange turn of phrase. It implies that was where they first met and got to know each other.

So why all the errors? Since Laura knew who the mail carrier was during the daring dash to Preston, having written about it in *The Long Winter*, it's curious that she stated Stella's family came the spring *after* the long winter. Some have speculated that she simply had misspoken one crucial word, perhaps meaning to say that they had arrived the spring *before* the long winter instead of *after*. Others wonder if she meant that David had come out prior to his family, so she was referring here to the rest of the Gilbert clan when she discussed their arrival.

Either way, it's curious to note that Laura is suggesting that she, and, tangentially, her family, didn't know the Gilberts before De Smet, and makes so many errors when describing her connection to them.

Whenever Stella arrived in town, and whichever way they were or weren't previously connected, however, Laura is crystal clear about one thing: Stella became a rival for Almanzo's affection. And Laura didn't like it one bit.

In "These Happy Golden Years," Laura describes her budding courtship with dashing homesteader, Almanzo James Wilder, who was almost exactly ten years her senior. Their relationship strengthened during sleigh rides home from Laura's first teaching assignment at the Brewster School (Bouchie School in real life), various "seeing-home" walks from social events, and long Sunday buggy rides through the prairie countryside. In chapter 20, "Nellie Oleson," Laura recounts her surprise when Almanza shows up one Sunday with Nellie in the seat next to him. Fictitious Nellie is clearly scheming to edge Laura out of the weekly drives, and succeeded in joining them for a couple of weeks, despite her fear of horses. A fuming Laura eventually gives Almanzo an ultimatum: he can take Nellie for a drive, or her, but not both. When Almanzo came alone to pick her up the next week, he confessed that he felt sorry for Nellie.

> I wouldn't have brought her the first time, but I overtook her walking in the road. She was walking all the way to town to see someone, but she said she'd rather go along with us. Sundays at

ong and lonely that I felt sorry for her. (These
Happy Golden Years, Ch. 20, "Nellie Oleson.")

This fictional version of how Nellie managed to insinuate herself into their private Sunday drives is pretty close to the "real"
story Laura described in *Pioneer Girl*:

> One Sunday we were coming home rather late on a road that
> led by our house first, so naturally I got out and Manly took
> Stella on home by herself. The next Sunday, he picked Stella
> up first as his farm was much nearer Gilbert's than ours. We
> went on South from our place to Lake Henry and again came
> back so that I stopped first.
>
> The next Sunday again Stella came with Manly after me. I
> went pleasantly enough, but Stella's smugness gave her scheme
> away to me. She was trying her best to edge me out of the
> drives. It was even more plain when she made plans for the
> next Sunday's drive and kindly (?) included me in them.
>
> . . . [After the following week's drive, in which Laura ensured
> Stella was dropped home first], Manly got out of the buggy and
> helped me down. As we stood there, Manly said, "Well, I sup-
> pose we'll all go next Sunday?"
>
> "No!" I answered. "We'll not all go. If you want Stella, take
> her. You need not think you have to come by for me. Good
> night!" and I went in and shut the door.
>
> . . . next Sunday . . . the brown horses came dashing around the
> corner . . . with Manly alone in the buggy and we did not go by
> for Stella nor was she mentioned on that afternoon. Neither was
> she included any more in our drives.

So the events leading up to Laura's ultimatum were pretty accurate, but was the reason Almanzo decided to bring Nellie along

Robynne Elizabeth Miller

in the first place equally as accurate? *Almost.*

As Laura had said, Ma Gilbert had taken to her bed, leaving Stella, the oldest Gilbert girl, to take care of the new baby, the younger children, the housework, and her ailing mother. This workload was why Almanzo felt so sorry for her. . .not merely because Sundays were long and lonely at their homestead. In *Pioneer Girl*, however, Laura wasn't fully buying in to Stella's claim to sympathy:

> Sometimes we [Laura and Manly] drove over to the Gilbert's and took Stella with us. Manly said the poor girl worked so hard it would be nice to give her a good time.
>
> I didn't object to her going with us but I did think of how she lay in bed in the morning and let her father get the breakfast, of how she was often too sick to work and lay in bed all day, but would get up at night and go to a dance. But I said nothing about all this. If she had worked on his sympathy, what did I care.

Ouch. With all due respect to Laura, I would say that she actually did, indeed, care. Very much! No matter how you read her words, that's a pretty scathing endorsement of Stella's character, or lack thereof! When we couple that with Laura's observation that Ma Gilbert "had not been out of her bed. . .though she looked well enough, with bright eyes and color in her cheeks," it appears that Laura wasn't particularly impressed with either Stella or Mrs. Gilbert. (*Pioneer Girl*)

This story about the buggy rides was the last mention of "Nellie Oleson" in any of the *Little House* books.

Early Life

Like Laura, Stella was also the product of a pioneering family. Estella M. Gilbert was born in May of 1864 in Lake City, Wabasha County, Minnesota, directly across Lake Pepin from Laura's "little house in the big woods." She was the third child and oldest daughter of Silliman Nathaniel Gilbert and Emily Jane Rundle.

Stella's extended family had come to Wabasha County, Minnesota, probably from Connecticut, where most of them were born. They settled in Mt. Pleasant Township, which was formally organized in "1858, and so named on account of the scenic overlooks from area summits," (Wikipedia) starting with her uncle, Sanford Gilbert, who arrived around 1855:

> In June, 1854, the settlement was begun by the location of A. A. Warren on the northwest quarter of section 1. He came with his family from Jo Daviess county, Illinois, ... In the fall [of 1855] Sanford Gilbert settled on the farm where he now lives. . . . The year 1857 saw quite an immigration, and the township rapidly filled up. (*History of Wabasha County*)

Sanford's obituary states that he arrived in Minnesota on October 1st, 1856, which contradicts the 1855 date of the above. Given the "History of Wabasha County" was written much closer to the time in question, and was a carefully researched recording of history, that's more likely to be correct. Either way, the Gilbert family showed a lot of perseverance in their new home, which was typical of the pioneers in those early years:

> Those who came with a supply of money got along well enough, but many who lacked ready cash, experienced considerable hardship. During the "winter of the deep snow" (1856-7) markets were often inaccessible, provisions rather scarce, and trust was not to be had by the moneyless. Stories are told of those who lived for weeks on potatoes and salt, or a similarly

scant diet, and one family is said to have existed four weeks on frozen rutabagas. Here, as elsewhere, the monotony of life was broken by visiting ox teams, merry gatherings, getting lost on the prairie, hunting, etc. and as the settlement grew older, and the virgin soil bestowed successive bounties on the brave pioneers, population and prosperity rapidly increased, and this little spot, but yesterday the home of the buffalo and Indian, has become one of the most desirable places in the county. (*History of Wabasha County*)

By all accounts, this area of Wabasha County was lovely. The township was located just west of Lake City, where Stella was born, as well as directly west across Lake Pepin from Laura's birthplace of Pepin, Wisconsin:

The appropriate name [Of Mt. Pleasant Township] was suggested by the magnificent view presented to an observer from the tops of some of the elevations in the south central part, and from the summit of Lone Mount [the highest point in the Twp] the sight is truly grand. For miles in all directions stretches the expanse of the prairie, whose fertility is attested by the neat and commodious buildings everywhere present; neat churches and schoolhouses add to the effect, while to the northeast the eye catches the river hills of the Wisconsin side, and a glimpse of the blue waters of Lake Pepin through the valley of Boodie creek. . . . (*History of Wabasha County*)

Much of Stella's family, being among the first settlers in the area, seemed deeply involved in the founding, development, and political history of the township and county. Her grandfather, Silas Gilbert, was among those tasked with naming the newly formed township, though his particular suggestion wasn't adopted:

> In the spring of 1858 a meeting was held at the residence of E. H. Palmer to determine the name of the township about to be organized. Several names were proposed, among them "Huntington" by Wm. Lewis, and "Greenfield," by Silas Gilbert, both seeking to honor places of former residence. After considerable debate the present name was adopted, as before mentioned, being suggested by the views the adjacent elevations commanded. (*History of Wabasha County*)

The Gilbert family's participation in civic duties didn't end with the formation and naming of Mt. Pleasant, however. Stella's father, Silliman, and, particularly, her uncle, Sanford, held various offices throughout the young township's formative years:

> May 11, 1858, the legal voters met at the house of Benj. Taylor, on section 32, twenty-three voters being present. . . . The men elected were the only candidates, having been chosen beforehand by mutual consent, and were voted for regardless of party.

> The result of the election is partly shown in the table given below, and besides these the following officers were chosen: J. W. Cross and Silliman Gilbert, assistant supervisors . . . .

Year	Chairman of Board	Assessor	Clerk	Treasurer
1861	---	---	Sanford Gilbert	---
1867	Sanford Gilbert	---	---	---
1868	---	Sanford Gilbert	---	---
1869	---	Sanford Gilbert	---	---
1871	Sanford Gilbert	---	---	---

(History of Wabasha County)

It's a little uncertain when the Gilberts moved across Lake Pepin, to the Ingalls side of the Mississippi River. We know that most of Stella's siblings were born in Minnesota, in the areas of

Lake City and Mount Pleasant. However, Elizabeth Ann Gilbert, who was born in 1875, is listed as having been born in Wisconsin in most censuses, as was Ada Mae Gilbert, who was born in 1876. As some Gilbert children were born in Minnesota, and some were born in Wisconsin, it seems more than reasonable to assume that the Gilberts moved to the Wisconsin side of Lake Pepin some time between September of 1870 (Charles' birth date) and September of 1875 (Elizabeth's birth date). Hazel Gilbert Falling, David Gilbert's daughter, confirmed in her interview with *LORE* magazine, that her grandparents (Silliman and Emily) had also lived in the Pepin area.

At some point in that timespan, the Ingalls were supposed to have attended the Barry Corner School at the same time as the Gilberts. Laura attended school briefly in the fall of 1871, but Mary continued on, probably until the Ingalls moved further west. It's unknown whether Laura started school again at Barry Corner before they left the area in May of 1874, but there were several school terms between the Gilbert's arrival in the area and the Ingalls' departure from it when the children could easily have been classmates for a second time.

Eventually, the Gilberts headed west again, leaving most of their extended family behind in the Pepin area. They stopped in the newly formed town of De Smet, South Dakota, and were listed as living there on the 1880 Federal Census. Laura, however, seemed to think the Gilberts came later. In *Pioneer Girl*, she noted that "they had come early in the spring after the hard winter." The Hard Winter was the winter of 1880-1881, so that would have meant Laura believed they had arrived in early spring, 1881. She was clearly off by a year, which could have simply been an error in memory or it could have been that she really meant to write "before" the hard winter, instead of "after."

Regardless of what Laura wrote, the Gilberts were in the area by the earlier date. In "By the Shores of Silver Lake," you'll remember that Reverend Alden happened by the Surveyor's House where the Ingalls had wintered and conducted what is considered the first religious service in the town of De Smet. That was on February 29th, 1880. In the spring of that year, still 1880, a more formal church was organized. It first met in the unfinished railroad depot, then, on June 20th, it was officially organized. One year later, in 1881, the church started raising funds for a building, and construction began in 1882, with Charles Ingalls helping with the project. The first meeting in the new church was held on August 30th, 1882. Silliman and Emily were part of this entire process, as noted by Daniel Zochert, in his book "Laura: The Life of Laura Ingalls Wilder:"

> Reverend Brown organized De Smet's first church, the First Congregational Church, at a meeting in the railroad depot. Boxes and boards were used as seats. Ma and Pa and Mary were founding members, along with Reverend Brown and his wife, Silliman M. Gilbert and his wife, and Vischer V. Barnes, a young lawyer from New York.

When you do the math, if Silliman and Emily were founding members, and were part of the group meeting in the railroad depot, the Gilberts had to have been there before June 20th, 1880, contrary to Laura's belief.

Married Life and Death

Marriages

John Seth Drury

Born 1857, Skellingthorpe, North Kesteven, Lincolnshire, England
Died 1895, De Smet, Kingsbury County, South Dakota, USA

Alva Merrill

Born 1853, West Virginia, USA
Died February 16th, 1920, Zillah, Yakima County, Washington, USA

Stella was married twice. Her first marriage was to John Seth Drury, who died when he was about thirty-six years old. There seems to be a little confusion about exact death dates, however. According to his headstone, John was born in the spring of 1857 and died, aged thirty-four, in 1891. But his son was born in December of 1893! As Stella was not an elephant with a two-year gestation, those dates simply don't add up. Mistakes were often made with birth, marriage, and death dates, even on grave stones, but this is an interesting one. Another, far more likely, and widely accepted, date of death is 1895.

John was an immigrant from Skellingthorpe, Lincolnshire, England and changed his name from Seth Booth Drury when emigrating to the United States in 1885, though it's not clear why. Using your middle name as your first wasn't unusual (think: David Allison "Al" Gilbert and Charles Frederick "Freddie" Ingalls), but dropping your legal first name and adding a new middle name was. According to his naturalization papers, he may also have used his brother's name, Charles Drury, for a short time, though why he would do that is yet another mystery. His father was Robert Drury and his mother was Hannah Booth Drury.

John had worked as a bootmaker in England and was the oldest of seven children. After arriving in the United States, he eventually settled in De Smet, where he met and married Stella. At one point, John worked at the roller mill in De Smet, a mill similar to the one his brother-in-law, Fred Gilbert, owned later. In May of 1892, John was mangled in the mill's gearing and he received severe injuries from the accident. He didn't die from his injuries, however, though the cause of his death a few years later is unknown and could, perhaps, be related. He died in De Smet when his first and only child, Fred Seth Drury, was very young, leaving Stella a twenty-nine-year-old widow and mother.

Stella and John's son, Fred Seth Drury, was born December 3rd, 1893, in De Smet.

Stella was listed as a widow at the time of the 1900 census, and was still living with her son, "Freddie," in De Smet. However, within a few years, Stella had embarked on the long westward journey to Yakima County, Washington. There, she met and married her second husband, Alva Merrill, in the town of Toppenish. The exact location of their meeting and courtship is uncertain, but the wedding took place in Stella's home on May 5th, 1906. Their marriage record indicates that Alva had also been living in Toppenish prior to their nuptials.

We know that Stella's father, Silliman, was living in nearby Buena by 1903, so perhaps she came west to be nearer her parents. Stella's sister, Luella, was a witness to her wedding, too, and she was living in the town of Zillah at the time. Buena, Zillah, and Toppenish are all within five miles of each other. The newly married couple were living in Zillah by 1910, which is the first time they appeared in a census together.

Prior to this, an "Estella Gilbert" is listed in the 1904 Polk's *Portland* (Oregon) City Directory, but we have no conclusive proof it's the same person. Stella's brother, Christopher, who sometimes went by his middle name, Lafayette, was living in Portland in 1904, which makes it possible that it's our Stella, and could explain part of her draw to the west coast. But these two listed Gilberts weren't living particularly near each other in Portland. If it was our Stella, it would seem a little odd that a single mother wouldn't be living a little closer to her brother, in such a large city. Especially if he was the reason she came out to that area prior to settling in Toppenish.

Alva was about four years older than Stella's first husband, having been born in 1853, and was a fruit farmer like most residents of Yakima County at that time. However, unlike Stella's first husband, John, Alva was an American by birth, born in what would eventually become West Virginia to Rawley and Nancy Merrill, who were also farmers.

By the time Alva was eight years old, he, his parents and four siblings were farming further west in Osage Township, Morgan County, Missouri. Alva later continued his parents' westward movements by ending up all the way out in Yakima County, Washington, where he became a successful fruit farmer.

In the November 2nd, 1904, edition of the *Yakima Herald*, it was reported that Alva, along with O. B. Whitson, had "started for the St. Louis fair last Friday [and] Mr. Merrill will spend the winter at his old home in north Missouri." The same newspaper, in its March 13th, 1907, edition, reported that "[a]mong those who are planting new orchards and enlarging their old ones are . . . Alva Merrill . . . ." At the time Alva was planting these new orchards, he and Stella had been married for about ten months.

By 1910, Alva and Stella, as well as Stella's son, Freddie, who was seventeen at the time, were living north of the Yakima River. This is the area in which they spent the rest of their married life. They lived in the towns of Zillah and Buena and continued fruit farming. Alva died at sixty-seven years old on February 16th, 1920.

At some point after Alva's death, Stella moved to Yakima City, where she was a lodger at 29 South 4th Street. However, as old-age progressed, she moved in with her younger sister, Elizabeth, back in Buena. Most of Stella's sisters were living in Yakima

County by this time, as well, so she was close to family when she died on September 16th, 1944, at the age of eighty.

Her obituary in the local paper read:

> Mrs. Estella Merrill, 80, died Saturday morning in Yakima. She was born in Minnesota and had lived in this community for 50 years. Members of her family included one son, Fred Drury of Seattle, a sister, Mrs. W. J. Morrision of Buena; two brothers, C. L. Gilbert of Union Gap and C. N. Gilbert of San Pedro, Cal.; one niece, Mrs. Martin Bjer of Yakima; a nephew, Charles Morrison of Zillah and one grand child. Langenvin-Meyer has charge of arrangements.

Family

Children

John and Stella had only one son: **Fred Seth Drury**, who was born December 3rd, 1893, in De Smet, Kingsbury County, South Dakota.

Though Freddie continued living with his mother and step-father into adulthood, some time before the 1920 Federal Census, he had moved to Pierce County, Washington, where he was living with his uncle, Charles Drury. Charles was his father's younger brother. Fred's uncle was a merchant tailor, with his own business, and in the 1920 census, where he and Freddie first appear together, Freddie is listed as a salesman tailor. So it's clear that Freddie moved in with his uncle to work for him and learn the tailoring business.

Fred was to eventually marry Ivy Bell Caldan on May 24th, 1924, in King County, Washington. Ivy was born in Grant County, South Dakota, on August 27th, 1897. They had one son, Caldan G. (Possibly Gilbert) Drury, born on April 29th, 1929. Fred was a veteran of World War 1.

City directories for Seattle and Tacoma indicate Fred continually worked in the tailoring business with other members of the Drury family. He appears to have started at twenty years old, in 1913, as a salesman. His Uncle Charles was President of the company, which was established in 1889. By 1917, Fred was still in Tacoma and was now secretary of "Drury the Tailor." In 1931 he had been promoted to the position of manager in a Seattle location, which implies they had opened a second branch by that time. By 1935 Fred was Vice-President of the company and, some time between 1943 and 1948, he had risen to President. He was still President in 1953.

However, he died quite far from Washington, in San Diego, California, on September 10th, 1964. Caldan had lived in the Palm

Springs area in the 1950's, so he and Ivy might have moved south to be closer to their son. Or they could have just been sick of the Pacific Northwest rain!

Interestingly, four years after Fred's death, his widow, Ivy, remarried at the age of seventy, to Richard B. Wagner (who was seven years her junior!) in San Diego. Ivy moved back to Washington at some point, probably following Caldan, who, at the time of this writing, was still alive. Ivy died on the 18th of January, 1988, in Kirkland, King County, Washington.

Grandparents

Stella's paternal grandparents were **Silas Gilbert and Marietta (or Maretta) Gould**. Silas was born 1806 in Fairfield County, Connecticut, and died in 1865, Wabasha County, Minnesota. He is buried in Gilbert Valley Cemetery, Wabasha County. His wife, Marietta, was born Jun 10th, 1815, in Fairfield County, Connecticut, and died Nov 10th, 1905, in Goodhue County, Minnesota. She is also buried in the Gilbert Valley Cemetery.

Stella's maternal grandparents were **William Oliver Rundle and Elizabeth May Edwards**. William was born on September 12th, 1815, in New Jersey. Elizabeth was born on January 2nd, 1818, also in New Jersey. They married on April 30th, 1837. William died on August 2nd, 1909, in Lake City, Minnesota, at the impressive age of ninety-three. Elizabeth died in 1893 in Lake City, Minnesota, at the age of seventy-five.

Parents

Stella's father was **Silliman Nathaniel Gilbert**, born December 25th, 1834, in Fairfield County, Connecticut, and died Apr 14th, 1921, in Zillah, Yakima County, Washington. He is buried in Tahoma Cemetery, Yakima County, Washington.

Stella's mother, **Emily Jane Rundle**, who was born August 16th, 1844, in Hawley, Pennsylvania, was a very, very young wife and mother. There are some discrepancies regarding dates, however. Her cemetery index card lists August 16th, 1844, as her birth date. Other documents disagree, citing a birth year of 1843, instead. On the 1900 Federal Census, Emily, herself, listed her birth year as 1843, and on the Minnesota Territorial Census, she gave her age as fourteen, which would correspond to an 1843 birth year. No matter which year was correct, however, she was extremely young to be tying the knot: she was only fourteen or fifteen years old when she married Silliman, who was roughly ten years her senior. Not only that, she was a first-time mother by fifteen or sixteen.

Prior to their marriage, in the Minnesota Territorial Census of 1857, which was conducted on September 21st, an Emily J. Rundle is listed as residing in Goodhue County with a large family, headed by David Vining. This doesn't make much sense at first glance as the poor girl would have only been a month past her thirteenth or fourteenth birthday, depending on which birth year you use. Some researchers have surmised that this meant she must have been an orphan, but that's not the case. Her mother and father were still very much alive, living in neighboring Wabasha County, just southeast of Goodhue.

Looking at the census entry, which consisted of David Vining, age forty-three, an "RS" Vining, age thirty-nine, and six children between the ages of two and sixteen (five of whom are males!), it's more than likely that Emily was a hired girl, brought in to help with all those young ones. Given she had approximately eight siblings herself, she would have had plenty of experience in household chores and managing younger children. And given how hard that must have been for such a young girl, getting married at roughly fifteen must have seemed like a wonderful way out of an overwhelming job.

Silliman and Emily had many healthy children, the first of which, Christopher Lafayette (often referred to as "Lafayette"), was born in Minnesota around December 1859, when Emily would have been only fifteen or sixteen years old! After Lafayette, there were seven more Gilbert children: David Allison ("Al)" (born in Minnesota in 1862), Estella M. (born in Minnesota in May of 1864), William Frederick ("Fred") (born in Minnesota in 1867), Charles Nathan (born in Minnesota in September of 1870), Elizabeth Ann (born in Wisconsin in 1875), Ada Mae (born in Wisconsin in 1876), and Luella B. (born in South Dakota in 1881).

Emily died March 16th, 1927, in Zillah, Yakima County, Washington.

Siblings

Christopher Lafayette Gilbert (1859-1947)

The oldest of the Gilbert siblings, Christopher Lafayette, who was born in Minnesota in November of 1859, initially stayed with the rest of his family after they moved to a township just outside of De Smet. There he farmed alongside his father and younger brother, David. However, around that time period, many residents of the De Smet area were being encouraged by the government to head west to the fertile land of the Pacific Northwest, especially Oregon. Christopher seemed up for the adventure so he packed up, left his family, and headed out. He had several adventures, even working for a time in Skagway during the Klondike gold rush as a jeweler, but eventually settled in the Yakima Valley near many of his family members.

Lafayette married Linda (Malinda) P. Wallace on December 3rd, 1904, when he was forty-five and she was thirty-five. Lafayette passed away at the age of eighty-seven, on October, 18th, 1947, in the town of Fairview, which is in the Union Gap/Yakima, Washington, area. He is buried in Tahoma Cemetery, Yakima County.

David Allison Gilbert (1862-1933)

Unlike the rest of his siblings, Stella's second older brother, David Allison "Al" Gilbert, remained in the De Smet area all his adult life. He was born in Wabasha County, Minnesota on May 22nd, 1862, and died in De Smet, South Dakota on May 16th, 1933, just six days short of his seventy-first birthday.

As a young man, Al worked as a mail carrier for a while and his major "Little House" claim to fame occurred in Laura's book, *The Long Winter*. In it, his daring trip between life-threatening blizzards to Preston, delivering and fetching the isolated town's mail, is featured. His second claim to fame did not appear in the *Little House* series: he was a pall-bearer at Mary Ingalls' funeral.

David was married to Sarah ("Sally") Lingby (also spelled Lingebye) who was born in Denmark.

William Frederick ("Fred") Gilbert (1867-1899)

Fred Gilbert was not only very close in age to Laura, being born on June 16th, 1867, but he was also born only a few miles from her, just across Lake Pepin in Lake City, Wabasha County, Minnesota. He was Silliman and Emily's fourth child, born three years after Stella.

Though Fred only got a few cursory mentions in the *Little House* series, it seems that Laura might have slightly downplayed his true importance to her as a young lady. Remember her quote in *Pioneer Girl*? The one where she said: "Now Fred was going to school and seemed to want to be very attentive to me." Later in life, when she was in her eighties, Laura finally admitted to having had an early crush on Fred:

> It was Fred, exactly Laura's . . . age, who held her true affection. In her eighties, Laura . . . laughingly admitted to a crush on Hazel's Uncle Fred, to who one of her girl friends was already smitten! (*LORE*, Vol. 6, No. 2)

So, was Fred REALLY attentive to her, or was that merely wishful thinking on her part, considering this quote implies that Fred seemed to be smitten with someone else? It would be fun to step back in time and see for ourselves.

In any case, Laura married Almanzo, and Fred ended up marrying Arianna Janssen Heeren in Ainsworth, Browns County, Nebraska on March 4th, 1892.

Sadly, Fred was to die at a very, very young age on September, 26th, 1899. He was only thirty-two years old when he succumbed to heart failure, brought on by Bright's Disease, an acute disease of the kidneys that can raise blood pressure. Fred is buried in De Smet cemetery, very close to members of the Ingalls family.

Charles Nathan Gilbert (1870-1955)

Charles was born on September 23rd, 1870, in Mount Pleasant, Wabasha County, Minnesota and moved with the family to De Smet. However, he was one of the most nomadic of the Gilbert children, living in several different locations along the west coast, from Washington down to California and back again. It was in Alameda County, California, though, that he met and married Anna Carolina Osborn on June 1st, 1898. Anna was born on October 13th, 1875.

Charles died in Seattle, King County, Washington, on March 11th, 1955. Even though his death certificate listed his age as eighty-three, he was actually eighty-four years old at the time of his death.

Elizabeth Ann Gilbert Morrison (1875-1945)

Stella was the oldest Gilbert daughter and was born right in the middle of four brothers. The next born, Elizabeth, was the sister closest in age but, even so, she was about eleven years younger than Stella, having been born in September of 1875 in Wisconsin. She married Wallace James Morrison (possibly called James Wallace as well, as per the 1880 census) sometime around 1893 or 1894, probably in De Smet, South Dakota (the whole Gilbert family was living in De Smet on the 1880 census and Elizabeth was still living there in 1900). Wallace was born on January 17th, 1866, in Ottumwa, Wapello County, Iowa.

Elizabeth died just fourteen months after Stella, on November 7th, 1945, in Buena, Yakima County, Washington. She's buried in the Tahoma Cemetery in Yakima City. Wallace died on April 21st, 1960 in Everett, Snohomish County, Washington.

Ada Mae Gilbert Folsom (1876-1928)

Ada was born in Wisconsin in November of 1876 and married Herbert Riley Folsom (1871-1941), probably in South Dakota, about 1896 or 1897. In the 1900 Census, she's living in De Smet on Third Street, next door to her parents, Silliman and Emily. Also on Third Street were the Ingalls family, including Charles, Caroline, Mary, Carrie, and Grace (Laura and Almanzo were married and in Mansfield, MO). Like the rest of her family, Ada and Herbert headed west, eventually settling in the Yakima Valley.

Ada died on September 4th, 1928, at the age of fifty, presumably in the Yakima area, as that is where she and Herbert were living in 1927 according to local city directories. Herbert died in Umatilla County, Oregon on March 6th, 1941. Both Elizabeth and Herbert are buried in the Tahoma Cemetery in Yakima, Washington.

Luella Belle Gilbert Sutherland (1881-1924)

Luella was the youngest of all the Gilbert children though, sadly, was also the first to die. She is also the one Laura mistakenly referred to as "Leona" in *Pioneer Girl*. Luella was born on August 8th, 1881, in De Smet, South Dakota. In 1900, at nineteen, she was still living with her parents in De Smet. At some point, Luella headed west as well. In Yakima County, Washington, at her parent's home, she married Jay L. Sutherland on November 3rd, 1912. Jay was born on November 7th, 1876, in Minnesota.

Luella died on March 21st, 1924, in Buena at only forty-two years old. Jay didn't die until March 24th, 1945, in San Luis Obispo, California. Both are buried in Tahoma Cemetery.

CONCLUSION

It would be easy to assume that anyone referenced in the creation of Nellie Oleson's character would HAVE to be an awful person. Right? I mean, if you add together everything Laura Ingalls Wilder wrote about Nellie throughout the *Little House* series, and in personal letters and writing notes, there's not much to appreciate, is there? Nellie was snooty, selfish, conniving, dishonest, and just plain rude.

But it wouldn't be entirely accurate to assume the real "Nellies" were as unredeemable as the *Little House* one. Nellie Oleson was a fictional character. . .a creation for the purpose of increasing narrative tension in a semi-autobiographical book series. Such creations can sometimes become one dimensional, even if they're brilliantly written. And even if they're based on actual people.

It's no secret that the real Laura didn't like the real Nellie, Genevieve, or Stella. But even Laura, herself, would probably recognize that even the most frustrating among us have some redeemable qualities. And that includes the three women she used to construct the composite character of Nellie Oleson.

Nellie Owens might have been piggish and petty as a child, but that's not necessarily who she grew into. We have to remember that Laura and Nellie parted ways while they were still very young—just children—so we shouldn't assume the immature Nellie Owens grew up to be an equally unpleasant adult.

Sure, there are some dodgy things we've discovered about Nellie. But right next to her divorce, untruths about her marital status, possible shady land deal, etc., were some human things, too. She was clearly loved by her children, for example, and was especially close to her daughter, Zola, with whom she often lived as an adult. And she experienced a lot of grief throughout her life via the loss of her mother, the mental deterioration of her father, her failed marriage, and tragically outliving her youngest son. It's difficult to fully dismiss a woman who crossed almost the entire country in her lifetime and had to deal with excruciating losses like that, even if she wouldn't let Laura play with her fancy toys as a child.

Genevieve Masters, however, is a little more difficult. Of the three "Nellies," she seems the hardest to fully excuse. After all, she wasn't a young, undisciplined child, as Nellie Owens was, when her extremely poor attitude was displayed. She was old enough to have known better than to be so snobbish and cutting, and certainly old enough to avoid earning the distinction of having "her tongue hung in the middle." Her meanness was a little more pointed, too. Calling Laura "fat?" Looking down at Cap Garland while hogging his candy? Difficult to defend this kind of behavior from a young lady her age.

But even then, if you look hard enough, her humanity comes through, too. Genevieve's only child was born twelve years into her marriage. As a woman who experienced ten years of fertility issues before my own biological son was born, that hits very close to home. Imagine what it must have felt like the day she was told, after more than a decade of marriage, that she was, finally, pregnant. It's hard to hate *that* Gennie. And, of course, how did she handle the embarrassment of her husband's incarceration? I wonder now, after getting to "know" her so much better, what her part in that incident was. Did she know and encourage his illegal activity? Or was she caught completely by surprise when William was arrested? Either way, how hard must that situation have been for a young woman in "delicate health," even if she participated in its creation? Given the fact that no prior or further illegal incidents occurred, we can assume that Gennie and William learned their lesson, and went on to behave respectfully thereafter.

I love, too, that after Gennie's premature death, William never married again. He was relatively young when she passed. . .only in his late forties to early fifties. He lived fifteen more years, and, though he had spent about thirty years in and around Chicago by that time, chose to be buried with Genevieve in De Smet. She stuck by him during his embezzlement troubles, and he remained faithful to her during more than a decade of infertility and after her death. I like to think that this shows that even Genevieve mellowed as she aged, perhaps helped by the love of her husband.

Estella Gilbert could be considered the most maligned in this trio, simply by a slightly unfair association. Laura never described Stella as a mean, selfish person, like she did Nellie and Gennie. Though it is true that Laura believed she was a little lazy. Remember Laura recounting that Stella often laid in bed in the morning, letting her father prepare breakfast, claiming she was unwell, yet got up and went to dances in the evening? That was a little unlikeable. But, aside from that, her only real "fault" was that she was interested in Almanzo, and may have tried to encourage his attentions. Can you blame her, though? He was an attractive young man and a bit of a catch in his day!

Stella's "buggy" story may have made it into *These Happy Golden Years*, but it would be wrong to assign either Nellie Owen's or Genevieve's countenance to her. She simply wasn't cut from the same snobby cloth. Her life after her brief *Little House* appearance had some hard times, too. Widowed twice, once in her late twenties with a young son to support, Stella had to find the courage and strength to pick herself up and keep moving forward. And she did. . .all the way to the west coast. Admirable, don't you think?

Laura once wrote that she was sure Nellie "was much more unhappy than she ever could have made" her. Whether she was talking about Nellie Owens, or the composite character she had created, it would certainly have been applicable to both Nellie Owens and Genevieve Masters. One was extremely unpleasant as a child, while the other was insufferable as a teenager/young adult. But both must have had some deep inner hurt or void which drove their nastier behaviors. Wounded people often try to wound others.

Stella didn't fit the disagreeable side of the "Nellie" persona, but she did contribute an important storyline for the budding romance of Almanzo and Laura. That makes her an important part of the character of Nellie Oleson, but not a defining one. Nellie Owens and Genevieve, however, combine for the lion's share of the *Little House* story lines and, sadly, for the more unpleasant attributes of Nellie Oleson's character.

Together, these three pioneer women make up one of the most iconic and enduring antagonists in literary history. Their lives individually, and collectively, are worth infinitely more than that, however. Nellie Owens, Genevieve Masters, and Estella Gilbert were remarkable as much for their own intriguing stories as for the part they played on the banks of Plum Creek, and in the western prairies of De Smet.

SOURCES

General Online Sources

Ancestry.com	http://home.ancestry.com/
ChicagoAncestors.org	http://www.chicagoancestors.org/
FamilySearch.org	https://familysearch.org/
FindAGrave.com	http://www.findagrave.com/
FindMyPast.com	http://www.findmypast.com/
FreeBMD	http://www.freebmd.org.uk/
Newspapers.com	https://www.newspapers.com/
Historic Oregon Newspapers	http://oregonnews.uoregon.edu/

Cemeteries

Forest View Cemetery (Forest Grove, Washington County, OR)
Tahoma Cemetery (Yakima, Yakima County, WA)
Zillah Cemetery (Zillah, Yakima County, WA)

Censuses Online[4]

U.S. Federal Censuses

United States Federal Census (1840)
United States Federal Census (1850)
United States Federal Census (1860)
United States Federal Census (1870)
United States Federal Census (1880)
United States Federal Census (1900)
United States Federal Census (1910)
United States Federal Census (1920)
United States Federal Census (1930)
United States Federal Census (1940)
United States Merchant Seamen Census (1930)

U.S. State and Territorial Censuses

Minnesota Territorial Census (1857)
Minnesota State Census (1875)
New York State Census (1865)
New York State Census (1875)
South Dakota State Census (1905)
South Dakota State Census (1915)

---

[4] Available on ancestry.com, familysearch.org & findmypast.com

South Dakota State Census (1925)
South Dakota State Census (1935)
South Dakota State Census (1945)
Washington Territorial Census (1889)

U.K. Censuses

England and Wales (1861)
England and Wales (1871)
England and Wales (1881)
Scotland Census (1851)
Scotland Census (1861)
Scotland Census (1871)

Libraries

Forest Grove City Library (Forest Grove, OR)
Multnomah County Library, Central Library (Portland, OR)
West Valley Library (Yakima, WA)

Historical/Genealogical Societies

Friends of Historic Forest Grove
Tillamook County Pioneer Museum
Yakima Valley Genealogical Society

Specific Sources

Amato, Lisa et al., *Images of America: Forest Grove*, [Arcadia Publishing], 2010, (p. 34), https://books.google.com/books?id=DvcIZv_6O84C&pg=PA34

Anderson, William (Ed.), *Little House Sampler*, "How Laura Got Even", [Harper Collins, NY], 1989, (pp. 19-23)

Anderson, William (Ed.), *Selected Letters of Laura Ingalls Wilder*, [Harper Collins, NY], 2016

Beaverton Times, "Kirry-Buchanan Wedding Announcement", Jul 2, 1920, (p. 4)

Beaverton Times, "Kirry-Galt Wedding Announcement", Nov 18, 1921, (p. 3), http://oregonnews.uoregon.edu/lccn/sn96088374/1921-11-18/ed-1/seq-3/

Bedal, Sheryl J., *Sheryl Jo Bedal's Family Tree: Information about Frank Lester (Bedal) Owens*, http://www.genealogy.com/ftm/b/e/d/Sheryl-J-Bedal/ WEBSITE-0001/UHP-0095.html

Buhler, Skip, Email correspondence regarding the Owens' land in Forest Grove, [Friends of Historic Forest Grove]

Bureau of Land Management, General Land Office Records, "Patent Details: Kirry, Nellie W/Owens, Nellie W. ", http:// www.glorecords.blm.gov/details/ patent/default.aspx?accession=OROCAA%20029551&docClass=SER& sid=t5cqaz4u.kb0

Bureau of Land Management, General Land Office Records, "Patent Details: Masters, Jesse F. B.", http://www.glorecords.blm.gov/details/patent/ default.aspx?accession=SDMTAA%20093263&docClass=SER& sid=sf1wiadi.za2

Bureau of Land Management, General Land Office Records, "Patent Details: Owens, William R.", http:// www.glorecords.blm.gov/details/patent/ default.aspx? accession=OROCAA%20029552&docClass=SER& sid=yxjpjfkw.4gs

Bureau of Land Management, General Land Office Records, http://www.glorecords.blm.gov/search/default.aspx

Bureau of Land Management, *Shaping America's History: The Homestead Act*, 2012, https://www.blm.gov/or/landsrealty/homestead150/files/ HomesteadingFactSheet_2012.pdf

California Marriage Records from Select Counties, 1850-1941, [Ancestry.com Operations, Inc.], 2014, http://search.ancestry.com/search/db.aspx?dbid=8797

California, Voter Registrations, 1900-1968, [Ancestry.com Operations, Inc.], 2008, http://search.ancestry.com/search/db.aspx?dbid=1249

Canada- Letters From The Front, 1920, [FindMyPast], http://search.findmypast.com/search-world-Records/canada--letters-from-the-front-1920

Cemetery Cards for Silliman Gilbert and Emily J. Gilbert, [Yakima Valley Genealogical Society]

Chicago, IL (1910), [ChicagoAncestors.org], http://www.chicagoancestors.org/sites/default/files/downloads/1910r.pdf

Church That Pa Built, [De Smet Alliance Church], http://desmetalliancechurch.com/about-us/the-church-that-pa-built/

Civil Registration Index of Births, Marriages and Deaths for England and Wales, [Free UK Genealogy], http://www.freebmd.org.uk

Clayton, W. W., *History of Steuben County, New York*, "Hornby", [Lewis, Peck & Co., Philadelphia], (pp. 313-316), https://archive.org/details/historyofsteuben00clay

Cleaveland, Nancy S., *Laura Ingalls Wilder and Education in Kingsbury County, Dakota Territory 1880-1885*, [Laura Ingalls Wilder Memorial Society, De Smet, SD], 2015

Cleveland High School: Cleveland's History, [Portland Public Schools], http://portland.schoolwires.net/Page/6694

Daily Capital Journal, "Police Save Then Arrest Salesman", Jul 24, 1937, (p. 9)

Daily Chronicle (Centralia, WA), "Fishermen Not Found", Mar 19, 1958, (p. 20)

de Carlo, Debbie, *Forest Grove Grave Draws 'Little House' Lovers*, [Portland-Tribune.com], Oct 8, 2014, http://portlandtribune.com/fgnt/36-news/236193-100930-forest-grove-grave-draws-little-house-lovers-

Dunbar, Charlene, *Re: Henry Sheard (1865)*, [Genealogy.com], Sep 28, 2008, http://www.genealogy.com/forum/regional/countries/topics/canada/83736/

Email from Yakima Valley Genealogical Society, "Obituary and Funeral Notices of Stillman N. Gilbert and Mrs. Emily Jane Gilbert"

Email from Yakima Valley Genealogical Society, "Obituary of Mrs. Estella Merrill"

Eugene Guard, "Going to Portland", May 27, 1921

Eugene Guard, "Junior High School", Sep 24, 1921

Eugene Guard, "Junior High Teacher Ill", Apr 23, 1921

Eugene Guard, "Lloyd P. Kirry Gold Pin Award", Jun 3, 1951, (p. 4)

Eugene Guard, "Obituary of Lloyd P. Kirry", Oct 13, 1961

Eugene Guard, "Portland Woman Visits Here", Jun 22, 1921

Eugene Guard, "Returns to School", Jan 3, 1922

Eugene Guard, "Spends Christmas with Family", Dec 24, 1920

Eugene Guard, "Teaching Corps Now Complete", May 21, 1920

Eugene Guard, "Visits Daughter in Eugene", Dec 6, 1920

Eugene Guard, Jul 9, 1921

Eugene Guard, Nov 24, 1920

Eugene Guard, Oct 10, 1940, (p. 5)

Eugene Guard, Oct 11, 1920

Eugene Register, Apr 1, 1930

FamilySearch, California Great Registers, 1866-1910, [FamilySearch], 2016, https://familysearch.org/search/collection/1935764

FamilySearch, California Marriage Index, 1960-1985, [FamilySearch], 2016

FamilySearch, United States World War II Draft Registration Cards, 1942, [FamilySearch], 2016, https://familysearch.org/search/collection/1861144

FamilySearch, Washington Death Certificates, 1907-1960, [FamilySearch], 2016, https://familysearch.org/search/collection/1454923

Fry-Matson, Ruby (Trsb.), Tillamook Herald, "Obituary of Margaret H. Owens", [Tillamook County Pioneer Museum], Feb 20, 1908, Transcript

Hill, Pamela Smith, *Laura Ingalls Wilder: A Writer's Life*, [South Dakota Historical Society Press], 2007

Hill, Pamela Smith (Ed.), *Pioneer Girl: The Annotated Autobiography*, [South Dakota Historical Society Press], 2014

Hines, Harvey K., *An Illustrated History of the State of Washington*, [The Lewis Publishing Company, Chicago, IL], 1893, https://archive.org/details/illustratedhisto00hine

History - Beaumont Village PDX, [BeaumontVillagePDX.com], http://www.beaumontvillagepdx.com/history/

History of Wabasha County: Together with Biographical Matter, Statistics, Etc. Vol 2, "Chapter LXXVII: Mount Pleasant Township", [H. H. Hill & Co.], 1884, (p. 752), https://books.google.com/books?id=-U80AQAAMAAJ&pg=PA752

HistoryLink.org, *The Free Online Encyclopedia of Washington State History*, http://www.historylink.org/

Hosford Middle School: Hosford's History, [Portland Public Schools], http://www.pps.net/Page/8866

House Journal of the Fifth Legislature of the State of Washington, [Washington State Printer], Jan 11, 1897, (p. 62), https://books.google.com/books?id=2SlNAAAAYAAJ&pg=PA62&lpg=PA62

Hughes County History, [Hughes County, South Dakota], http://hughescounty.org/about/history/

Humboldt County, California Biographies: Joseph Bransetter, [The CAGenWeb Project], http://www.cagenweb.com/humboldt/bios/Humb.1025-1290.htm

Illinois Deaths and Stillbirths Index, 1916-1947, [Ancestry.com Operations, Inc.], 2011, http://search.ancestry.com/search/db.aspx?dbid=2542

Irvington School (Portland, Oregon), [Oregon Digital], https://oregondigital.org/catalog/oregondigital:df67rn72v#page/1/mode/1up

Ketcham, Sallie, *Laura Ingalls Wilder: American Writer on the Prairie*, [Routledge], 2014

Lake City Graphic, "Obituary of Sanford Gilbert", [Ancestry.com Operations, Inc.], Dec 9, 1902, http://mv.ancestry.com/viewer/e039217a-e359-4abd-af19-04ff2e0cf3c0/16557252/393231884

Lawson, Tracy, *Lessons From Laura: Creating Nellie Oleson*, qtg Wilder, Laura Ingalls, *Pioneer Girl* (unpublished), Apr 3, 2013, http://tracylawsonbooks.com/228/

Marriage Return of Alva Merrill and Estella Drury, [Washington State Digital Archives], http://digitalarchives.wa.gov/WA.Media/jpeg/ED200AEAE8CA72F709CD55675D3BB777_1.jpg

Miller, John E., *Becoming Laura Ingalls Wilder: The Woman Behind the Legend*, [University of Missouri], 2006

Minnesota Official Marriage System, https://www.moms.mn.gov/Search

Morning Oregonian, Feb 26, 1895, (p. 3)

Morning Oregonian, Feb 12, 1909, (p. 16)

Morning Register, "Geary Junior High", Apr 10, 1921

Morning Register, "Teaching Personnel of City Schools Announced", May 26, 1921

Morning Register, "To Investigate Y.W.C.A.", Mar 7, 1922

Morning Register, Sep 25, 1921

Mount Pleasant Township, Wabasha County, Minnesota, [Wikipedia], https://en.wikipedia.org/wiki/Mount_Pleasant_Township,_Wabasha_County,_Minnesota

Nicolai, Dianna, The LeRoy Independent, "Nellie Oleson of 'Little House on the Prairie' ~A native of 'Old Town' LeRoy", Mar 25, 2010, (pp. 1 & 13), http://lry.stparchive.com/Archive/LRY/LRY03252010p001.php & http://lry.stparchive.com/Archive/LRY/LRY03252010p013.php

Oakland Tribune, Jun 1, 1898, (p. 3)

One Room School, [Herbert Hoover Presidential Library Museum], https://hoover.archives.gov/LIW/DeSmet/desmet_oneroomschool.html

Oregon Births & Baptisms 1868-1929, [FindMyPast], http://www.findmypast.com/articles/world-records/full-list-of-united-states-records/birth-marriage-and-death/oregon-births-and-baptisms-1868-1929

Oregon Daily Journal, "Normal School to Hold Exercises on Next Wednesday", Jun 13, 1920

Oregon Daily Journal, Jun 12, 1919

Oregon Daily Journal, Sep 10, 1920

Oregon Death Index, 1903-1998, [FamilySearch],
https://familysearch.org/search/collection/1946790

Oregon Historical Records Index, "Kirry, Nellie W. v Kirry, H.F.", [Oregon Secretary of State Archives Division],
http://genealogy.state.or.us/detail.php?id=582066

Oregon Historical Records Index, "Owens, Philadelphia Ann vs Owens, Willie R.", [Oregon Secretary of State Archives Division],
http://genealogy.state.or.us/detail.php?id=511425

Oregon State Hospital, [Wikipedia],
https://en.wikipedia.org/wiki/Oregon_State_Hospital

Oregon, Motor Vehicle Registrations, 1911-1946, [Ancestry.com Operations, Inc.], http://search.ancestry.com/search/db.aspx?dbid=1852

Oregon, Washington and Alaska gazetteer and business directory : 1901-1902, [Ancestry.com Operations, Inc.],
http://search.ancestry.com/search/db.aspx?dbid=27625

Oregon's Forgotten Hospital, [OregonLive.com], Apr 3, 2013,
http://www.oregonlive.com/editors/index.ssf/2013/04/
oregons_forgotten_hospital.html

Person Details for Oswald Kirry, "Illinois, County Marriages, 1810-1934", [FamilySearch], https://familysearch.org/ark:/61903/1:1:QK9L-QY15

Peterson, Daniel D. , *Chronicle of Walnut Station*, [Lulu.com], 2014

Peterson, Daniel D., *What Happened to Those People Laura Ingalls Wilder Wrote About?*, [Lulu.com], 2013

Port Angeles Evening News (Port Angeles, WA), "Two Anglers Missing", Mar 19, 1958

Portland City Directory (1902), [R. L. Polk & Co.]

Portland City Directory (1903), [R. L. Polk & Co.]

Portland City Directory (1904), [R. L. Polk & Co.]

Portland City Directory (1905), [R. L. Polk & Co.]

Portland City Directory (1906), [R. L. Polk & Co.]

Portland City Directory (1907-08), [R. L. Polk & Co.]

Portland City Directory (1907-1908), [R. L. Polk & Co.]

Portland City Directory (1909), [R. L. Polk & Co.]

Portland City Directory (1909), [R. L. Polk & Co.]

Portland City Directory (1910), [R. L. Polk & Co.]

Portland City Directory (1910), [R. L. Polk & Co.]

Portland City Directory (1911), [R. L. Polk & Co.]

Portland City Directory (1911), [R. L. Polk & Co.]

Portland City Directory (1912), [R. L. Polk & Co.]

Portland City Directory (1912), [R. L. Polk & Co.]

Portland City Directory (1913), [R. L. Polk & Co.]

Portland City Directory (1925), [R. L. Polk & Co.]

Portland City Directory (1930), [R. L. Polk & Co.]

Portland City Directory (1934), [R. L. Polk & Co.]

Portland City Directory (1939), [R. L. Polk & Co.]

Portland City Directory (1940), [R. L. Polk & Co.]

Portland City Directory (1942), [R. L. Polk & Co.]

Portland City Directory (1943-44), [R. L. Polk & Co.]

Rachel Regina Zimmerman Samuels, [FamilySearch], Nov 2, 2013, https://familysearch.org/photos/artifacts/3219360

Robinson, Doane, *History of South Dakota*, Vol. II, [B. F. Bowen & Co.], 1904, (p. 1097-1099), https://books.google.com/books?id=UptQAAAAYAAJ

South Dakota Birth Index, 1856-1915, [Ancestry.com Operations, Inc.], http://search.ancestry.com/search/db.aspx?dbid=6996

Statesman Journal (Salem, OR), "Bay City Items", May 20, 1891

Statesman Journal (Salem, OR), "Bay City Items", May 28, 1891

Tillamook County Marriages 1891-1895, [OrGenWeb], http://www.rootsweb.ancestry.com/~ortillam/htm/marriage_records/1891-1895.htm

Transactions of the California State Agricultural Society During the Year 1888, [State Office, Sacramento, CA], 1889, https://books.google.com/books?id=RLZAAQAAMAAJ

U.S. City Directories, 1822-1995 [database on-line], [Ancestry.com Operations, Inc.], 2011, http://search.ancestry.com/search/db.aspx?dbid=2469

U.S., Social Security Applications and Claims Index, 1936-2007, [Ancestry.com Operations, Inc.], 2015, http://search.ancestry.com/search/db.aspx?dbid=60901

U.S., World War I Draft Registration Cards, 1917-1918, [Ancestry.com Operations, Inc.], 2005, http://search.ancestry.com/search/db.aspx?dbid=6482

U.S., World War II Army Enlistment Records, 1938-1946, [Ancestry.com Operations, Inc.], 2005, http://search.ancestry.com/search/db.aspx?dbid=8939

U.S., World War II Army Enlistment Records, 1938-1946, [Ancestry.com Operations, Inc.], 2005, http://search.ancestry.com/search/db.aspx?dbid=8939

Ukiah Daily Journal (Ukiah, CA), "Obituary of Oswald Kirry ('Death of An Old Citizen')", Sep 28, 1906, (p. 1)

United States Social Security Death Index, https://familysearch.org/search/collection/1202535

Upham, Warren, *Minnesota Place Names: Geographical Encyclopedia*, 3rd Edition, [Minnesota Historical Society Press], 2001

Washington Death Certificates, 1907-1960, [FamilySearch], https://familysearch.org/search/collection/1454923

Washington Digital Archives, Yakima County Auditor, Marriage Records, 1896-2008, [Washington State Archives], http://www.digitalarchives.wa.gov/Collections/TitleInfo/21

Washington, Seattle Passenger Lists, 1890-1957, http://www.findmypast.com/articles/world-records/full-list-of-united-states-records/immigration-and-travel/washington-seattle-passenger-lists-1890-1957

Waskin, Laura, *Best of the LORE*, "Nellie Oleson Story Continues", [Laura Ingalls Wilder Memorial Society, De Smet, SD], 2007, (pp. 60-61)

Waskin, Laura, *Best of the LORE*, "Nellie Oleson: Lost and Found", [Laura Ingalls Wilder Memorial Society, De Smet, SD], 2007, (pp. 57-59)

West, Andrew Fleming, *Monographs on Education in the United States*, Vol. 5, "The American College", [J. B. Lyon Company], 1904, (p. 42), https://books.google.com/books?id=AKM-AQAAMAAJ&pg=PA42

Wilder, Laura Ingalls, *By the Shores of Silver Lake*

Wilder, Laura Ingalls, Handwritten letter to the third and fourth grades at Forston School, May 22, 1949

Wilder, Laura Ingalls, *Little Town on the Prairie*

Wilder, Laura Ingalls, *On the Banks of Plum Creek*

Wilder, Laura Ingalls, *The Long Winter*

Wilder, Laura Ingalls, *These Happy Golden Years*

Willamette Valley, Oregon, Death Records, 1838-2006, "Terwilliger Funeral Home Records, Vol. D #131", [Willamette Valley Genealogical Society/ Ancestry.com Operations, Inc], 1998/2012, http:// interactive.ancestry.com/ 2468/40289_1821100517_0744-00106?pid=1667

Yakima Herald, Mar 13, 1907

Yakima Herald, Nov 2, 1904

Zochert, Donald, *Laura: The Life of Laura Ingalls Wilder*, [Avon Books, NY], 1976

ABOUT THE AUTHOR

Robynne Elizabeth Miller is wife to an amazing Brit, mother to a glorious brood of adopted and biological kids, and makes her home in the snowy woods of Northern California's Sierra Nevada Mountains.

Besides her own writing, Robynne speaks on a variety of topics, teaches at writing conferences and other venues, leads two writing groups, is a private writing coach, and serves on the Board of Directors of Inspire Christian Writers.

Passionate about her family, faith, music and cooking, she can also be found blogging at mylittleprairiehome.com and thepracticalpioneer.com.

Email

robynne@thepracticalpioneer.com

Web

mylittleprairiehome.com & thepracticalpioneer.com

Twitter

@mlprairiehome

Pinterest

pinterest.com/mlprairiehome/

OTHER BOOKS BY
ROBYNNE ELIZABETH MILLER

From the Mouth of Ma:
A Search for Caroline Quiner Ingalls

There's not a whole lot written about Caroline Quiner Ingalls, the mother of famed *Little House on the Prairie* author, Laura Ingalls Wilder. And I always wondered why.

So I set about looking for her. . .in family letters, bits of biography and, mostly, through the words she spoke throughout the *Little House* series.

The Ma I thought I'd find wasn't the one I discovered. Would you like to meet her? I think you'll be happy that you did.

Pioneer Mixology

Don't get your knickers in a knot. . .this isn't a bartender's how-to or seedy guide to saloon life in the mid-1800's! Not on your Nellie!

Pioneer Mixology is just a quirky guide to the beverages available in that time period. It's a mix of history, settler ingenuity, and, yes, even some recipes.

Learn how to make Ma Ingalls' ginger water, party beverages from curdled milk (yuck!!), and why, on earth, they used to put egg shells or the swim bladder of a sturgeon in their coffee!